BOSTON, 135 WASHINGTON STREET,
SEPTEMBER, 1851.

NEW BOOKS AND NEW EDITIONS

PUBLISHED BY

TICKNOR, REED, AND FIELDS.

HENRY W. LONGFELLOW'S WRITINGS.

THE GOLDEN LEGEND. A Mystery. Price $1.00.

POETICAL WORKS. This edition contains the six Volumes mentioned below, and is the only complete collection in the market. In two volumes, 16mo, $2.00.

In separate Volumes, each 75 cents.

VOICES OF THE NIGHT.
BALLADS AND OTHER POEMS.
SPANISH STUDENT; A PLAY IN THREE ACTS.
BELFRY OF BRUGES, AND OTHER POEMS.
EVANGELINE; A TALE OF ACADIE.
THE SEASIDE AND THE FIRESIDE.
THE WAIF. A Collection of Poems. Edited by Longfellow.
THE ESTRAY. A Collection of Poems. Edited by Longfellow.

MR. LONGFELLOW'S PROSE WORKS.

HYPERION. A ROMANCE. Price $1.00.

OUTRE-MER. A PILGRIMAGE. Price $1.00.

KAVANAGH. A TALE. Price 75 cents.

NATHANIEL HAWTHORNE'S WRITINGS.

TWICE-TOLD TALES. Two Volumes. Price $1.50.

THE SCARLET LETTER. Price 75 cents.

THE HOUSE OF THE SEVEN GABLES. Price $1.00.

TRUE STORIES FROM HISTORY AND BIOGRAPHY. With fine Engravings. Price 75 cents.

A WONDER BOOK FOR BOYS AND GIRLS. With fine Engravings. Price 75 cents.

JOHN G. WHITTIER'S WRITINGS.

OLD PORTRAITS AND MODERN SKETCHES. Price 75 cents.

MARGARET SMITH'S JOURNAL. Price 75 cents.

SONGS OF LABOR, AND OTHER POEMS. Price 50 cts.

OLIVER WENDELL HOLMES'S WRITINGS.

POETICAL WORKS. With fine Portrait. Price $1.00.

ASTRÆA. Price 25 cents.

ALFRED TENNYSON'S WRITINGS.

POETICAL WORKS. With Portrait. 2 vols. Price $1.50.

THE PRINCESS. Price 50 cents.

IN MEMORIAM. Price 75 cents.

THOMAS DE QUINCEY'S WRITINGS.

CONFESSIONS OF AN ENGLISH OPIUM-EATER, AND SUSPIRIA DE PROFUNDIS. Price 75 cents.

BIOGRAPHICAL ESSAYS. Price 75 cents.

MISCELLANEOUS ESSAYS. Price 75 cents.

THE CÆSARS. Price 75 cents.

LIFE AND MANNERS. Price 75 cents.

LITERARY REMINISCENCES. 2 Vols. Price $1.50.

GRACE GREENWOOD'S WRITINGS.

GREENWOOD LEAVES. 1st & 2d Series. Price $1.25 each.

POETICAL WORKS. With fine Portrait. Price 75 cents.

HISTORY OF MY PETS. With fine Engravings. Price 50 cents.

RECOLLECTIONS OF MY CHILDHOOD. With fine Engravings.

EDWIN P. WHIPPLE'S WRITINGS.

ESSAYS AND REVIEWS. 2 Vols. Price $2.00.

LECTURES ON SUBJECTS CONNECTED WITH LITERATURE AND LIFE. Price 63 cents.

WASHINGTON AND THE REVOLUTION. Price 20 cts.

HENRY GILES'S WRITINGS.

LECTURES, ESSAYS, AND MISCELLANEOUS WRITINGS. 2 Vols. Price $1.50.

CHRISTIAN THOUGHT ON LIFE. Price 75 cents.

WILLIAM MOTHERWELL'S WRITINGS.

POEMS, NARRATIVE AND LYRICAL. Price 75 cents.

POSTHUMOUS POEMS. Price 50 cents.

MINSTRELSY, ANCIENT AND MODERN. 2 Vols. Price $1.50.

JAMES RUSSELL LOWELL'S WRITINGS.

COMPLETE POETICAL WORKS. Revised, with Additions. In two volumes, 16mo. Price $1.50.

SIR LAUNFAL. Price 25 cents.

MISCELLANEOUS.

WILLIAM WORDSWORTH'S BIOGRAPHY. By Dr. C. WORDSWORTH. 2 Vols. Price $2.50.

ROBERT BROWNING. COMPLETE POETICAL WORKS. 2 Vols. Price $2.00.

BARRY CORNWALL. ENGLISH SONGS AND OTHER SMALL POEMS. Enlarged Edition. $1.00.

RICHARD MONCKTON MILNES. POEMS OF MANY YEARS. Price 75 cents.

PHILLIP JAMES BAILEY. THE ANGEL WORLD AND OTHER POEMS. Price 50 cents.

GOETHE'S WILHELM MEISTER. Translated by CARLYLE. 2 Vols. Price $2.50.

GOETHE'S FAUST. Price 75 cents.

CHARLES SPRAGUE. Poetical and Prose Writings. With fine Portrait. Price 75 cents.

CHARLES SUMNER. Orations and Speeches. 2 Vols. Price $2.50.

GEORGE S. HILLARD. The Dangers and Duties of the Mercantile Profession. Price 25 cents.

HORACE MANN. A Few Thoughts for a Young Man. Price 25 cents.

HENRY T. TUCKERMAN. Poems. Price 75 cents.

F. W. P. GREENWOOD. Sermons of Consolation. Price $1.00.

BAYARD TAYLOR. Poems. (Nearly ready.)

R. H. STODDARD. Poems. (Nearly ready.)

JOHN G. SAXE. Poems. Price 50 cents.

REJECTED ADDRESSES. By Horace and James Smith. Price 50 cents.

WARRENIANA. By the Authors of Rejected Addresses. Price 63 cents.

MEMORY AND HOPE. A Book of Poems, referring to Childhood. Price $2.00.

ALDERBROOK. By Fanny Forester. 2 Vols. Price $1.75.

HEROINES OF THE MISSIONARY ENTERPRISE. Price 75 cents.

MEMOIR OF THE BUCKMINSTERS, Father and Son. By Mrs. Lee. $1.25.

THE SOLITARY OF JUAN FERNANDEZ. By the Author of Picciola. Price 50 cents.

THE BOSTON BOOK. Price $1.25.

ANGEL-VOICES. Price 38 cents.

FLORENCE, AND OTHER TALES. By Mrs. Lee.

SIR ROGER DE COVERLEY. (Nearly ready.)

EACH OF THE ABOVE POEMS AND PROSE WRITINGS, MAY BE HAD IN VARIOUS STYLES OF HANDSOME BINDING.

A BOOK

OF

ROMANCES, LYRICS, AND SONGS,

BY

BAYARD TAYLOR.

BOSTON:
TICKNOR, REED, AND FIELDS.
M DCCC LII.

CAMBRIDGE:

METCALF AND COMPANY,

PRINTERS TO THE UNIVERSITY.

CONTENTS.

ROMANCES.

LYRICS.

SONGS AND SONNETS.

ROMANCES.

H. D. Scott.

MON-DA-MIN;

OR, THE ROMANCE OF MAIZE.

I.

Long ere the shores of green America
Were touched by men of Norse and Saxon blood,
What time the Continent in silence lay,
A solemn world of forest and of flood,
Where Nature wantoned wild in zones immense,
Unconscious of her own magnificence;

II.

Then to the savage race, who knew no world
Beyond the hunter's lodge, the council-fire,
The clouds of grosser sense were sometimes furled,
And spirits came to answer their desire,—
The spirits of the race, grotesque and shy;
Exaggerated powers of earth and sky.

III.

For Gods resemble whom they govern : they,
The fathers of the soil, may not outgrow
The children's vision. In that earlier day,
They stooped the race familiarly to know ;
From Heaven's blue prairies they descended then,
And took the shapes and shared the lives of men.

IV.

A chief there was, who in the frequent stress
Of want, yet in contentment, lived his days ;
His lodge was built within the wilderness
Of Huron, clasping those transparent bays,
Those deeps of unimagined crystal, where
The bark canoe seems hung in middle air.

V.

There, from the lake and from the uncertain chase
With patient heart his sustenance he drew ;
And he was glad to see, in that wild place,
The sons and daughters that around him grew,
Although more scant they made his scanty store,
And in the winter moons his need was sore.

VI.

The eldest was a boy, a silent lad,
Who wore a look of wisdom from his birth;
Such beauty, both of form and face, he had,
As until then was never known on earth,
And so he was (his soul so bright and far!)
Osséo named, — Son of the Evening Star.

VII.

This boy by nature was companionless;
His soul drew nurture only when it sucked
The savage dugs of Fable; he could guess
The knowledge other minds but slowly plucked
From out the heart of things; to him, as well
As to his Gods, all things were possible.

VIII.

The heroes of that shapeless faith of his
Took life from him: when gusts of powdery snow
Whirled round the lodge, he saw Paup-puckewiss
Floundering amid the drifts, and he would go
Climbing the hills, while sunset faded wan,
To seek the feathers of the Rosy Swan.

IX.

He knew the lord of serpent and of beast,
The crafty Incarnation of the North;
He knew, when airs grew warm and buds increased,
The sky was pierced, the Summer issued forth,
And when a cloud concealed some mountain's crest,
The Bird of Thunder brooded on his nest.

X.

Through Huron's mists he saw the enchanted boat
Of old Mishosha to his island go,
And oft he watched, if on the waves might float,
As once, the Fiery Plume of Wassamo;
And when the moonrise flooded coast and bay,
He climbed the headland, stretching far away;

XI.

For there — so ran the legend — nightly came
The small Puck-wudjees, ignorant of harm:
The friends of Man, in many a sportive game
The nimble elves consoled them for the charm
Which kept them exiled from their homes afar, —
The silver lodges of a twilight star.

XII.

So grew Osséo, as a lonely pine,
That knows the secret of the wandering breeze,
And ever sings its canticles divine,
Uncomprehended by the other trees:
And now the time drew nigh, when he began
The solemn fast whose issue proves the man.

XIII.

His father built a lodge the wood within,
Where he the appointed space should duly bide,
Till such propitious time as he had been
By faith prepared, by fasting purified,
And in mysterious dreams allowed to see
What God the guardian of his life would be.

XIV.

The anxious crisis of the Spring was past,
And warmth was master o'er the lingering cold.
The alder's catkins dropped; the maple cast
His crimson bloom, the willow's downy gold
Blew wide, and softer than a squirrel's ear
The white-oak's foxy leaves began appear.

XV.

There was a motion in the soil. A sound
Lighter than falling seeds, shook out of flowers,
Exhaled where dead leaves, sodden on the ground,
Repressed the eager grass ; and there for hours
Osséo lay, and vainly strove to bring
Into his mind the miracle of Spring.

XVI.

The wood-birds knew it, and their voices rang
Around his lodge ; with many a dart and whirr
Of saucy joy, the shrewish cat-bird sang
Full-throated, and he heard the kingfisher,
Who from his God escaped with rumpled crest,
And the white medal still upon his breast.

XVII.

The aquilegia sprinkled on the rocks
A scarlet rain ; the yellow violet
Sat in the chariot of its leaves ; the phlox
Held spikes of purple flame in meadows wet,
And all the streams with vernal-scented reed
Were fringed, and streaky bells of miskodeed.

XVIII.

The boy went musing: what are these, that burst
The sod and grow, without the aid of man?
What father brought them food? what mother nursed
Them in her earthy lodge, till Spring began?
They cannot speak; they move but with the air;
Yet souls of evil or of good they bear.

XIX.

How are they made, that some with wholesome juice
Delight the tongue, and some are charged with death?
If spirits them inhabit, they can loose
Their shape sometimes, and talk with human breath:
Would that in dreams one such would come to me,
And thence my teacher and my guardian be!

XX.

So, when more languid with his fast, the boy
Kept to his lodge, he pondered much thereon,
And other memories gave his mind employ;
Memories of winters when the moose were gone,—
When tales of Manabozo failed to melt
The hunger-pang his pining brothers felt.

XXI.

He thought : the Mighty Spirit knows all things,
Is master over all. Could He not choose
Design His children food to ease the stings
Of hunger, when the lake and wood refuse ?
If He will bless me with the knowledge, I
Will for my brothers fast until I die.

XXII.

Four days were sped since he had tasted meat ;
Too faint he was to wander any more,
When from the open sky, that, blue and sweet,
Looked in upon him through the lodge's door,
With quiet gladness he beheld a fair
Celestial Shape descending through the air.

XXIII.

He fell serenely, as a wingèd seed
Detached in summer from the maple bough ;
His glittering clothes unruffled by the speed,
The tufted plumes unshaken on his brow :
Bright, wonderful, he came without a sound,
And like a burst of sunshine struck the ground.

XXIV.

So light he stood, so tall and straight of limb,
So fair the heavenly freshness of his face,
Osséo looked with beating heart at him,
For now a God had visited the place.
More brave a God his dreams had never seen :
The stranger's garments were a shining green,

XXV.

Sheathing his limbs in many a stately fold,
That, parting on his breast, allowed the eye
To note beneath, his vest of scaly gold,
Whereon the drops of slaughter, scarcely dry,
Disclosed their blushing stain : his shoulders fair
Gave to the wind long tufts of silky hair.

XXVI.

The plumy crest, that high and beautiful
Above his head its branching tassels hung,
Shook down a golden dust, while, fixing full
His eyes upon the boy, he loosed his tongue.
Deep in his soul Osséo did rejoice
To hear the reedy music of his voice :

XXVII.

"By the Great Spirit I am hither sent.
He knows the wishes whereupon you feed, —
The soul, that, on your brothers' good intent,
Would sink ambition to relieve their need:
This thing is grateful to the Master's eye,
Nor will His wisdom what you seek, deny.

XXVIII.

"But blessings are not free; they do not fall
In listless hands; by toil the soul must prove
Its steadfast purpose master over all,
Before their wings in pomp of coming move:
Here, wrestling with me, must you overcome,
In me, the secret, — else, my lips are dumb."

XXIX.

No match for his, Osséo's limbs appeared,
Weak with the fast; and yet in soul he grew
Composed and resolute, by accents cheered,
That spoke in light what he but darkly knew.
He rose, unto the issue nerved; he sent
Into his arms the hope of the event.

XXX.

The shining stranger wrestled long and hard,
When, disengaging weary limbs, he said :
"It is enough ; with no unkind regard
The Master's eye your toil hath visited.
He bids me cease ; to-day let strife remain,
But on the morrow I will come again."

XXXI.

And on the morrow came he as before,
Dropping serenely down the deep-blue air :
More weak and languid was the boy, yet more
Courageous he, that crowning test to bear.
His soul so wrought in every fainting limb,
It seemed the cruel fast had strengthened him.

XXXII.

Again they grappled, and their sinews wrung
In desperate emulation ; and again
Came words of comfort from the stranger's tongue
When they had ceased. He scaled the heavenly plain,
His tall, bright stature lessening as he rose,
Till lost amid the infinite repose.

XXXIII.

On the third day descending as before,
His raiment's gleam surprised the silent sky;
And weaker still the poor boy felt, yet more
Courageous he, and resolute to die,
So he might first the promised good embrace,
And leave a blessing unto all his race.

XXXIV.

This time with intertwining limbs they strove;
The God's green mantle shook in every fold,
And o'er Osséo's heated forehead drove
His silky hair, his tassel's dusty gold,
Till, spent and breathless, he at last forbore,
And sat to rest beside the lodge's door.

XXXV.

" My friend," he said, " the issue now is plain;
Who wrestles in his soul must victor be;
Who bids his life in payment shall attain
The end he seeks — and you will vanquish me.
Then, these commands fulfilling, you shall win
What the Great Spirit gives in Mon-da-Min.

XXXVI.

" When I am dead, strip off this green array,
And pluck the tassels from my shrivelled hair;
Then bury me where summer rains shall play
Above my breast, and sunshine linger there.
Remove the matted sod; for I would have
The earth lie lightly, softly on my grave.

XXXVII.

" And tend the place, lest any noxious weed
Through the sweet soil should strike its bitter root;
Nor let the blossoms of the forest breed,
Nor the wild grass in green luxuriance shoot;
But when the earth is dry and blistered, fold
Thereon the fresh and dainty-smelling mould.

XXXVIII.

" The clamoring crow, the blackbird swarms that make
The meadow trees their hive, must come not near;
Scare thence all hurtful things; nor quite forsake
Your careful watch, until the woods appear
With crimson blotches deeply dashed and crossed,—
Sign of the fatal pestilence of Frost.

XXXIX.

" This done, the secret, into knowledge grown,
Is yours for evermore." With that, he took
The yielding air. Osséo, left alone,
Followed his flight with hope-enraptured look.
The pains of hunger fled ; a happy flame
Danced in his heart until the trial came.

XL.

It happened so, as Mon-da-Min foretold :
Osséo's soul, at every wreathing twist
Of palpitating muscle, grew more bold,
And from the limbs of his antagonist
Celestial vigor to his own he drew,
Till with one mighty heave he overthrew.

XLI.

Then from the body, beautiful and cold,
He stripped the shining clothes ; but on his breast
He left the vest, engrained with blushing gold,
And covered him in decent burial-rest.
At sunset to his father's lodge he passed,
And soothed with meat the anguish of his fast.

XLII.

Naught did he speak of all that he had done,
But day by day in secrecy he sought
An opening in the forest, where the sun
Warmed the new grave: so tenderly he wrought,
So lightly heaped the mould, so carefully
Kept all the place from choking herbage free,

XLIII.

That in a little while a folded plume
Pushed timidly the covering soil aside,
And, fed by fattening rains, took broader room,
Until it grew a stalk, and rustled wide
Its leafy garments, lifting in the air
Its tasselled top, and knots of silky hair.

XLIV.

Osséo marvelled to behold his friend
In this fair plant; the secret of the Spring
Was his at length; and till the Summer's end
He guarded him from every harmful thing.
He scared the cloud of blackbirds, wheeling low;
His arrow pierced the reconnoitring crow.

XLV.

Now came the brilliant mornings, kindling all
The woody hills with pinnacles of fire ;
The gum's ensanguined leaves began to fall,
The buckeye blazed in prodigal attire,
And frosty vapors left the lake at night
To string the prairie grass with spangles white.

XLVI.

One day, from long and unsuccessful chase
The chief returned. Osséo through the wood
In silence led him to the guarded place,
Where now the plant in golden ripeness stood.
"Behold, my father!" he exclaimed, "our friend,
Whom the Great Spirit unto me did send

XLVII.

"Then, when I fasted, and my prayer He knew,
That He would save my brothers from their want ;
For this, His messenger I overthrew,
And from his grave was born this glorious plant.
'T is Mon-da-Min : his sheathing husks inclose
Food for my brothers in the time of snows.

XLVIII.

"I leave you now, my father! Here befits
Me longer not to dwell. My pathway lies
To where the West Wind on the mountain sits,
And the Red Swan beyond the sunset flies:
There may superior wisdom be in store."
And so he went, and he returned no more.

XLIX.

But Mon-da-Min remained, and still remains;
His children cover all the boundless land,
And the warm sun and frequent mellow rains
Shape the tall stalks and make the leaves expand.
A mighty army they have grown: he drills
Their green battalions on the summer hills.

L.

And when the silky hair hangs crisp and dead,
Then leave their rustling ranks the tasselled peers,
In broad encampment pitch their tents instead,
And garner up the ripe autumnal ears:
The annual storehouse of a nation's need,
From whose abundance all the world may feed.

LOVE AND SOLITUDE.

I.

Earth knew no deeper life since Earth began,
And scarce the Heaven above :
For us the world contains no ban ;
In the profoundest measure given to Man,
We love, we love !
O, in that sound, completion lies
For all imperfect destinies.
It is a pulse of joy, that rings
The marriage-peal of Nature, brings
The lonely heart, the humblest and the least,
To share her royal feast ;
No more an outcast on her sod
Or at her board a stinted guest,
But now in purple raiment dressed
And heir to all delight, that she receives of God !

II.

A balmy breath is breathed upon the land,
And through the spirit's inmost cells
It floats and swells,
Till at the touch of its persuading hand
The jealous bolts give way, and every door
Stands wide for evermore.
Not only there, dear love, not only there
Where Love's warm chambers front the morning air,
Thy soul may walk, and in the secret bower
Where burns the holiest fire that Heaven lets fall,
And with Ambition, in his blazoned hall,
Hope, in her airy tower!
The heart has other guests than these,
More secret halls, more solemn mysteries.
Dark crypts, beheld of none,
Throne darker powers, that flee the sun,
Chained far below, and heard at intervals
When all is still, and through the trembling walls
Some guilty whisper calls;
Or, when the storms have blown
And the house rocks upon its basement stone,
They wring their chains with clamor that appals
The pale-cheeked lord. To thee
Those awful crypts and corridors are free.
Thou through the darkened hush mayst glide,

White and serene, with unaffrighted breath,
Past the blind Sins, that slumber leaden-eyed
In caves that lead to Death.
Nor I the less, where purer powers control
The perfect temple of thy soul,
And saintly harmonies to me
Breathe from its gates unceasingly,
Its bowery courts and chambers that infold
The chastened gleam of pearl and gold,
Free to the sun and blessed air :
No deeper gloom than starry twilight there !

III.

What is the world of men to us ? We love,
And Love hath his own world. Love hath
Repose in storms and peace in wrath,
Far from the shocks of Time a quiet path,
Another Earth below, another Heaven above.
Men from their weakness and their sin create
The iron bonds of State,
Soldered with wrongs of olden date, —
The heartless frame, the chance-directed law
Which grows to them a grand, avenging Fate,
And fills their darkness with its awe.
States have no soul. The World's tired brain
O'er many riddles broods with pain,

Not hopeless all, but hoping much in vain.
Those who have never loved may stay,
And in his files fight out the day ;
But aliens we, who breathe a separate air
In regions far away !
Thou art my law, I thine : the links we wear,
If not of Freedom, dearer still,
And binding both in one harmonious will.
Why should we track the labyrinth of ill
Before us, — mingle with the fret
Of jangling natures, till our souls forget
Their crystal orbits of accordant sound ?
Why should we walk the common ground,
Where gloom is born of gloom, and pain
From pain unfoldeth ever,
When to the blue air's limitless domain,
Made ours by right of love, we rise without endeavor ?

IV.

Some voice of wind or sea
May reach the imbruted slave, and in his ear
Drop Freedom's mighty secret: so to me
Through blindness and through passion came the clear,
Calm voice of Love, thenceforth to be
The revelation of diviner truth
Than ever touched our sinless youth, —

A power to bid us face Eternity!
But the same whisper that reveals the glory
Of Freedom's brow, makes also known
The bitterness of bondage. We
Will leave this splendid misery,
This hollow joy, whose laugh but hides a groan,
And teach our lives to write a perfect story.

V.

O, somewhere, in the living realms that lie
Between the icy zones of desolation,
Covered by some remote, unconscious sky,
Where God's serene creation
Yet never glassed itself in human eye,
Must be a glorious Valley, hidden
In the safe bosom of the hills that part
The river-veins of some old Continent's heart,
To love like ours a shelter unforbidden!
Some Valley must there be,
Of which wide wastes of desert sand have kept
The gateway secret, mountain walls
Across the explorer's pathway stepped,
Or mighty woods surrounded like a sea.
Love's voice, whene'er he calls,
Alike the compass to his freedom is,
And to that Vale, the lode-star of our bliss,

Our hearts shall guide us. Even now,
I see the close defiles unfold
Upon a sloping mead that lies below
A mountain black with pines,
O'er which the barren ridges heave their lines,
And high beyond, the snowy ranges old!
Fed by the plenteous mountain rain,
Southward, a blue lake sparkles, whence outflows
A rivulet's silver vein,
Awhile meandering in fair repose,
Then caught by riven cliffs that guard our home
And flung upon the outer world in foam!
The sky above that still retreat,
Through all the year serene and sweet,
Drops dew that finds the daisy's heart,
And keeps the violet's tender lids apart:
All winds that whistle drearily
Around the naked granite, die
With many a long, melodious sigh
Among the pines; and if a tempest seek
The summits cold and bleak,
He does but shift the snow from shining peak to peak.

VI.

Or should this Valley seem
Too deeply buried from the golden sun,

Still may a home be won
Whose breast lies open to his every beam.
Some Island, on the purple plain
Of Polynesian main,
Where never yet the adventurer's prore
Lay rocking near its coral shore :
A tropic mystery, which the enamored Deep
Folds, as a beauty in a charmèd sleep.
There lofty palms, of some imperial line,
That never bled their nimble wine,
Crowd all the hills, and out the headlands go
To watch on distant reefs the lazy brine
Turning its fringe of snow.
There, when the sun stands high
Upon the burning summit of the sky,
All shadows wither : Light alone
Is in the world : and, pregnant grown
With teeming life, the trembling island-earth
And panting sea forebode sweet pains of birth
Which never come, — their love brings never forth
The Human Soul they lack alone !

VII.

We to that Island soul and voice will be,
When (rapturous hour !) the baffling quest is over,
The boat is wrecked, the ship is blown to sea,

And underneath the palm-tree's cover
We bless our God that He hath left us free.
Then, wandering through the inland dells
Where sun and dew have built their gorgeous bowers,
The golden, blue, and crimson flowers
Will drain in joy their spicy wells,
The lily toll her alabaster bells,
And some fine influence, unknown and sweet,
Precede our happy feet
Around the Isle, till all the life that dwells
In leaf and stem shall feel it, and awake,
And even the pearly-bosomed shells
Wet with the foamy kiss of lingering swells,
Shall rosier beauty at our coming take,
For Love's dear sake !
There when, like Aphrodite, Morn
From the ecstatic waves is born,
The chieftain Palm, that tops each mountain-crest,
Shall feel her glory gild his scaly greaves,
And lift his glittering leaves
Like arms outspread, to take her to his breast.
Then shall we watch her slowly bend, and fold
The Island in her arms of gold,
Breathing away the heavy balms which crept
All night around the bowers, and lifting up
Each flower's enamelled cup,

To drink the sweetness gathered while it slept.
Yet on our souls a joy more tender
Shall gently sink, when sunset makes the sky
One burning sheet of opalescent splendor,
And on the deep dissolving rainbows lie.
No whisper shall disturb
That alchemy superb,
Whereto our beings every sense surrender.
O, long and sweet, while sitting side by side,
Looking across the western sea,
That dream of Death, that morn of Heaven, shall be ;
And when the shadows hide
Each dying flush, upon the quiet tide, —
Quiet as is our love, —
We first shall see the stars come out above,
And after them, the slanting beams that run,
Based on the sea, far up the shining track
Of the emblazoned Zodiac,
A pyramid of light, above the buried sun !

VIII.

There shall our lives to such accordance grow
As love — love true as ours — alone can know ;
Can never know but there :
Each within each involved, like Light and Air,
In endless marriage. Earth will fill

Her bounteous lap with all we ask of Earth,
Nor ever drought or dearth
Shrink the rich pulps of vale and hill.
Content at last the missing tone to hear
Through all her summer-chords,
Which makes their full-strung harmony complete
In her delighted ear,
Her dumb affection, voluble as words,
Shall to our hearts that harmony repeat.
Led by the strain, it may be ours to enter
The secret chamber where she works alone
With Color, Form, and Tone,
In human mood, or, sterner grown,
Takes hold on powers that shake her fiery centre.
Year after year the Island shall become
A fairer and serener home,
And happy children, beautiful as Dawn,
The future parents of a race
Whose purer eyes shall face to face
Look on the Angels, fill our place,
And be the Presence and the Soul, when we have gone.

IX.

Forgive the dream. Love owns no human birth,
And may not find fulfilment here
On this degenerate Earth.

Forgive the dream : here never yet was given
More than the promise and the hope of Heaven.
The dearest joy is dashed with fear,
Our darkest sorrow may be then most near.
Even with the will our passion lends
We cannot break the chain ;
Against our vows, we must remain
With common men, and compass common ends.
We cannot shut our hearts from haunting fears ;
We cannot purge our eyes from heavy tears ;
We cannot shift the burden and the woe
Which all alike must know,
Which Love's Elected through the countless years
Have known, and, knowing, died : God wills it so.

X.

Sit near me, then, and place thy hand in mine ;
Look on me with thine eyes, that I may feel
Thy love through all my being shine,
Until I glow with many a dream divine
Of larger freedom, — thus to steal
From this perplexed, unkindly strand,
And breathe the peace of some enamoring land.
Fear not to follow : Death
Is here, and Pain, and sobbing breath ;
But souls so blent may reach some radiant spot

Where these are not:
One isle is ours, that lies asleep
Upon an angel-guarded deep,
Where alien bark may never touch the shore, —
Thine, mine alone, for evermore!
There we are free in truth, there only free,
There only happy, lifted far above
Strange laws of men, not made for such as we,
For whom all founts of Nature overflow:
And Love hath bid us know,
All things are justified to those who love.

HYLAS.

STORM-WEARIED Argo slept upon the water.
No cloud was seen ; on blue and craggy Ida
The hot noon lay, and on the plain's enamel ;
Cool, in his bed, alone, the swift Scamander.
" Why should I haste ? " said young and rosy Hylas :
" The seas were rough, and long the way from Colchis.
Beneath the snow-white awning slumbers Jason,
Pillowed upon his tame Thessalian panther ;
The shields are piled, the listless oars suspended
On the black thwarts, and all the hairy bondsmen
Doze on the benches. They may wait for water,
Till I have bathed in mountain-born Scamander."

So said, unfilleting his purple chlamys,
And putting down his urn, he stood a moment,
Breathing the faint, warm odor of the blossoms
That spangled thick the lovely Dardan meadows.

Then, stooping lightly, loosened he his buskins
And felt with shrinking feet the crispy verdure,
Naked, save one light robe, that from his shoulder
Hung to his knee, the youthful flush revealing
Of warm, white limbs, half-nerved with coming manhood,
Yet fair and smooth with tenderness of beauty.
Now to the river's sandy marge advancing,
He dropped the robe and raised his head exulting
In the clear sunshine, that with beam embracing
Held him against Apollo's glowing bosom.
For sacred to Latona's son is Beauty,
Sacred is Youth, the joy of youthful feeling.
A joy indeed, a living joy, was Hylas,
Whence Jove-begotten Hêraclês, the mighty,
To men though terrible, to him was gentle,
Smoothing his rugged nature into laughter
When the boy stole his club, or from his shoulders
Dragged the huge paws of the Nemæan lion.
The thick, brown locks, tossed backward from his fore-
head,
Fell soft about his temples; manhood's blossom
Not yet had sprouted on his chin, but freshly
Curved the fair cheek, and full the red lip's parting,
Like a loose bow, that just has launched its arrow;
His large blue eyes, with joy dilate and beamy,
Were clear as the unshadowed Grecian heaven;

Dewy and sleek his dimpled shoulder rounded
To the white arms and whiter breast between them.
Downward, the supple lines had less of softness :
His back was like a god's ; his loins were moulded
As if some pulse of power began to waken ;
The springy fulness of his thighs, outswerving,
Sloped to his knee, and, lightly dropping downward,
Drew the curved lines that breathe, in rest, of motion.

Musing a space he stood, a light smile playing
Upon his face, — a spirit new-created
To the free air and all-embracing sunlight.
He saw his glorious limbs reversely mirrored
In the still wave, and stretched his foot to press it
On the smooth sole that answered at the surface :
Alas ! the shape dissolved in glimmering fragments.
Then, timidly at first, he dipped, and catching
Quick breath, with tingling shudder, as the waters
Swirled round his thighs, and deeper, slowly deeper,
Till on his breast the River's cheek was pillowed,
And deeper still, till every shoreward ripple
Talked in his ear, and like a cygnet's bosom
His white, round shoulder shed the dripping crystal.
There, as he floated, with a rapturous motion,
The lucid coolness folding close around him,
The lily-cradling ripples murmured : " Hylas ! "

He shook from off his ears the hyacinthine
Curls, that had lain unwet upon the water,
And still the ripples murmured: "Hylas! Hylas!"
He thought: "The voices are but ear-born music.
Pan dwells not here, and Echo still is calling
From some high cliff that tops a Thracian valley:
So long mine ears, on tumbling Hellespontos,
Have heard the sea-waves hammer Argo's forehead,
That I misdeem the fluting of this current
For some lost nymph —" Again the murmur: "Hy-
las!"
And with the sound a cold, smooth arm around him
Slid like a wave, and down the clear, green darkness
Glimmered on either side a shining bosom, —
Glimmered, uprising slow; and ever closer
Wound the cold arms, till, climbing to his shoulders,
Their cheeks lay nestled, while the purple tangles
Their loose hair made, in silken mesh enwound him.
Their eyes of clear, pale emerald then uplifting,
They kissed his neck with lips of humid coral,
And once again there came a murmur: "Hylas!
O, come with us, O, follow where we wander
Deep down beneath the green, translucent ceiling, —
Where on the sandy bed of old Scamander
With cool white buds we braid our purple tresses,
Lulled by the bubbling waves around us stealing.

Thou fair Geek boy, O, come with us! O, follow
Where thou no more shalt hear Propontis riot,
But by our arms be lapped in endless quiet,
Within the glimmering caves of Ocean hollow!
We have no love; alone, of all the Immortals,
We have no love. O, love us, we who press thee
With faithful arms, though cold, — whose lips caress thee, —
Who hold thy beauty prisoned. Love us, Hylas!"
The sound dissolved in liquid murmurs, calling
Still as it faded: "Come with us, O, follow!"
The boy grew chill to feel their twining pressure
Lock round his limbs, and bear him, vainly striving,
Down from the noonday brightness. "Leave me, Naiads!
Leave me!" he cried; "the day to me is dearer
Than all your caves deep-sphered in Ocean's quiet.
I am but mortal, seek but mortal pleasure:
I would not change this flexile, warm existence,
Though swept by storms and shocked by Jove's dread thunder,
To be a king beneath the dark-green waters."
Still moaned the humid lips, between their kisses:
"We have no love. O, love us, we who press thee!"
And came in answer, thus, the words of Hylas:
"My love is mortal. For the Argive maidens

I keep the kisses which your lips would ravish.
Unlock your cold, white arms, — take from my shoulder
The tangled swell of your bewildering tresses.
Let me return: the wind comes down from Ida,
And soon the galley, stirring from her slumber,
Will fret to ride where Pelion's twilight shadow
Falls o'er the towers of Jason's sea-girt city.
I am not yours, — I cannot braid the lilies
In your wet hair, nor on your argent bosoms
Close my drowsed eyes to hear your rippling voices.
Hateful to me your sweet, cold, crystal being,
Your world of watery quiet: — Help, Apollo!
For I am thine: thy fire, thy beam, thy music,
Dance in my heart and flood my sense with rapture:
The joy, the warmth and passion now awaken,
Promised by thee, but erewhile calmly sleeping.
O, leave me, Naiads! loose your chill embraces,
Or I shall die, for mortal maidens pining."
But still with unrelenting arms they bound him,
And still, accordant, flowed their watery voices:
"We have thee now, we hold thy beauty prisoned; —
O, come with us beneath the emerald waters!
We have no love; we love thee, rosy Hylas.
O, love us, who shall nevermore release thee:
Love us, whose milky arms will be thy cradle

Far down on the untroubled sands of ocean,
Where now we bear thee, clasped in our embraces."
And slowly, slowly, sank the amorous Naiads ;
The boy's blue eyes, upturned, looked through the
water,
Pleading for help ; but Heaven's immortal Archer
Was swathed in cloud. The ripples hid his forehead,
And last, the thick, bright curls a moment floated,
So warm and silky that the stream upbore them,
Closing reluctant, as he sank for ever.
The sunset died behind the crags of Imbros.
Argo was tugging at her chain ; for freshly
Blew the swift breeze, and leaped the restless billows.
The voice of Jason roused the dozing sailors,
And up the ropes was heaved the snowy canvas.
But mighty Hêraclês, the Jove-begotten,
Unmindful stood, beside the cool Scamander,
Leaning upon his club. A purple chlamys
Tossed o'er an urn was all that lay before him :
And when he called, expectant : "Hylas ! Hylas !"
The empty echoes made him answer : "Hylas !"

KUBLEH;

A STORY OF THE ASSYRIAN DESERT.

THE black-eyed children of the Desert drove
Their flocks together at the set of sun.
The tents were pitched ; the weary camels bent
Their suppliant necks, and knelt upon the sand ;
The hunters quartered by the kindled fires
The wild boars of the Tigris they had slain,
And all the stir and sound of evening ran
Throughout the Shammar camp. The dewy air
Bore its full burden of confused delight
Across the flowery plain, and while, afar,
The snows of Koordish Mountains in the ray
Flashed roseate amber, Nimroud's ancient mound
Rose broad and black against the burning West.
The shadows deepened and the stars came out,
Sparkling in violet ether ; one by one

Glimmered the ruddy camp-fires on the plain,
And shapes of steed and horseman moved among
The dusky tents with shout and jostling cry,
And neigh and restless prancing. Children ran
To hold the thongs while every rider drove
His quivering spear in the earth, and by his door
Tethered the horse he loved. In midst of all
Stood Shammeriyah, whom they dared not touch, —
The foal of wondrous Kubleh, to the Sheik
A dearer wealth than all his Georgian girls.

But when their meal was o'er, — when the red fires
Blazed brighter, and the dogs no longer bayed, —
When Shammar hunters with the boys sat down
To cleanse their bloody knives, came Alimàr,
The poet of the tribe, whose songs of love
Are sweeter than Bassora's nightingales, —
Whose songs of war can fire the Arab blood
Like war itself: who knows not Alimàr?
Then asked the men: "O Poet, sing of Kubleh!"
And boys laid down the burnished knives and said:
"Tell us of Kubleh whom we never saw, —
Of wondrous Kubleh!" Closer flocked the group,
With eager eyes, about the flickering fire,
While Alimàr, beneath the Assyrian stars,
Sang to the listening Arabs:

"God is great!
O Arabs, never yet since Mahmoud rode
The sands of Yemen, and by Mecca's gate
That wingèd steed bestrode, whose mane of fire
Blazed up the zenith, when, by Allah called,
He bore the Prophet to the walls of Heaven,
Was like to Kubleh, Sofuk's wondrous mare:
Not all the milk-white barbs, whose hoofs dashed flame,
In Bagdad's stables, from the marble floor, —
Who, swathed in purple housings, pranced in state
The gay bazars, by great Al-Raschid backed:
Not the wild charger of Mongolian breed
That went o'er half the world with Tamerlane:
Nor yet those flying coursers, long ago
From Ormuz brought by swarthy Indian grooms
To Persia's kings, — the foals of sacred mares,
Sired by the fiery stallions of the sea!

"Who ever told, in all the Desert Land,
The many deeds of Kubleh? Who can tell
Whence came she, whence her like shall come again?
O Arabs, sweet as tales of Scheherazade
Heard in the camp, when javelin shafts are tried
On the hot eve of battle, are the words
That tell the marvels of her history.

" Far in the Southern sands, the hunters say,
Did Sofuk find her, by a lonely palm.
The well had dried ; her fierce, impatient eye
Glared red and sunken, and her slight young limbs
Were lean with thirst. He checked his camel's pace,
And while it knelt, untied the water-skin,
And when the wild mare drank, she followed him.
Thence none but Sofuk might the saddle gird
Upon her back, or clasp the brazen gear
About her shining head, that brooked no curb
From even him ; for she, alike, was royal.

" Her form was lighter, in its shifting grace,
Than some impassioned almée's, when the dance
Unbinds her scarf, and golden anklets gleam,
Through floating drapery, on the buoyant air.
Her light, free head was ever held aloft ;
Between her slender and transparent ears
The silken forelock tossed ; her nostril's arch,
Thin-blown, in proud and pliant beauty spread,
Snuffing the desert winds. Her glossy neck
Curved to the shoulder like an eagle's wing,
And all her matchless lines of flank and limb
Seemed fashioned from the flying shapes of air.
When sounds of warlike preparation rang
From tent to tent, her keen and restless eye

Shone blood-red as a ruby, and her neigh
Rang wild and sharp above the clash of spears.

"The tribes of Tigris and the Desert knew her:
Sofuk before the Shammar bands she bore
To meet the dread Jebours, who waited not
To bid her welcome; and the savage Koord,
Chased from his bold irruption on the plain,
Has seen her hoof-prints in his mountain snow.
Lithe as the dark-eyed Syrian gazelle,
O'er ledge and chasm and barren steep amid
The Sinjar hills, she ran the wild ass down.
Through many a battle's thickest brunt she stormed,
Reeking with sweat and dust, and fetlock deep
In curdling gore. When hot and lurid haze
Stifled the crimson sun, she swept before
The whirling sand-spout, till her gusty mane
Flared in its vortex, while the camels lay
Groaning and helpless on the fiery waste.

"The tribes of Taurus and the Caspian knew her:
The Georgian chiefs have heard her trumpet neigh
Before the walls of Teflis; pines that grow
On ancient Caucasus have harbored her,
Sleeping by Sofuk in their spicy gloom.
The surf of Trebizond has bathed her flanks,

When from the shore she saw the white-sailed bark
That brought him home from Stamboul. Never yet,
O Arabs, never yet was like to Kubleh!

"And Sofuk loved her. She was more to him
Than all his snowy-bosomed odalisques.
For many years she stood beside his tent,
The glory of the tribe.

"At last she died.
Died, while the fire was yet in all her limbs, —
Died for the life of Sofuk, whom she loved.
The base Jebours — on whom be Allah's curse! —
Came on his path, when far from any camp,
And would have slain him, but that Kubleh sprang
Against the javelin points, and bore them down,
And gained the open Desert. Wounded sore,
She urged her light limbs into maddening speed,
And made the wind a laggard. On and on
The red sand slid beneath her, and behind
Whirled in a swift and cloudy turbulence,
As when some star of Eblis, downward hurled
By Allah's bolt, sweeps with its burning hair
The waste of darkness. On and on the bleak,
Bare ridges rose before her, came and passed,
And every flying leap with fresher blood

Her nostril stained, till Sofuk's brow and breast
Were flecked with crimson foam. He would have
turned
To save his treasure, though himself were lost,
But Kubleh fiercely snapped the brazen rein.
At last, when through her spent and quivering frame
The sharp throes ran, our clustering tents arose,
And with a neigh, whose shrill excess of joy
O'ercame its agony, she stopped and fell.
The Shammar men came round her as she lay,
And Sofuk raised her head and held it close
Against his breast. Her dull and glazing eye
Met his, and with a shuddering gasp she died.
Then like a child his bursting grief made way
In passionate tears, and with him all the tribe
Wept for the faithful mare.

"They dug her grave
Amid Al-Hather's marbles, where she lies
Buried with ancient kings; and since that time
Was never seen, and will not be again,
O Arabs, though the world be doomed to live
As many moons as count the desert sands,
The like of glorious Kubleh. God is great!"

METEMPSYCHOSIS OF THE PINE.

As when the haze of some wan moonlight makes
  Familiar fields a land of mystery,
Where all is changed, and some new presence wakes
    In flower, and bush, and tree, —

Another life the life of Day o'erwhelms;
  The Past from present consciousness takes hue,
And we remember vast and cloudy realms
    Our feet have wandered through :

So, oft, some moonlight of the mind makes dumb
  The stir of outer thought : wide open seems
The gate wherethrough strange sympathies have come,
    The secret of our dreams ;

The source of fine impressions, shooting deep
Below the failing plummet of the sense;
Which strike beyond all Time, and backward sweep
Through all intelligence.

We touch the lower life of beast and clod,
And the long process of the ages see
From blind old Chaos, ere the breath of God
Moved it to harmony.

All outward wisdom yields to that within,
Whereof nor creed nor canon holds the key;
We only feel that we have ever been
And evermore shall be;

And thus I know, by memories unfurled
In rarer moods, and many a nameless sign,
That once in Time, and somewhere in the world,
I was a towering Pine,

Rooted upon a cape that overhung
The entrance to a mountain gorge; whereon
The wintry shadow of a peak was flung,
Long after rise of sun.

Behind, the silent snows; and wide below,
The rounded hills made level, lessening down
To where a river washed with sluggish flow
A many-templed town.

There did I clutch the granite with firm feet,
There shake my boughs above the roaring gulf,
When mountain whirlwinds through the passes beat,
And howled the mountain wolf.

There did I louder sing than all the floods
Whirled in white foam adown the precipice,
And the sharp sleet that stung the naked woods
Answer with sullen hiss:

But when the peaceful clouds rose white and high
On blandest airs that April skies could bring,
Through all my fibres thrilled the tender sigh,
The sweet unrest of Spring.

She, with warm fingers laced in mine, did melt
In fragrant balsam my reluctant blood;
And with a smart of keen delight I felt
The sap in every bud,

And tingled through my rough old bark, and fast
  Pushed out the younger green, that smoothed my tones,
When last year's needles to the wind I cast
    And shed my scaly cones.

I held the eagle, till the mountain mist
  Rolled from the azure paths he came to soar,
And like a hunter, on my gnarled wrist
    The dappled falcon bore.

Poised o'er the blue abyss, the morning lark
  Sang, wheeling near in rapturous carouse,
And hart and hind, soft-pacing through the dark,
    Slept underneath my boughs.

Down on the pasture-slopes the herdsman lay,
  And for the flock his birchen trumpet blew;
There ruddy children tumbled in their play,
    And lovers came to woo.

And once an army, crowned with triumph, came
  Out of the hollow bosom of the gorge,
With mighty banners in the wind aflame,
    Borne on a glittering surge

Of tossing spears, a flood that homeward rolled,
  While cymbals timed their steps of victory,
And horn and clarion from their throats of gold
    Sang with a savage glee.

I felt the mountain-walls below me shake,
  Vibrant with sound, and through my branches poured
The glorious gust: my song thereto did make
    Magnificent accord.

Some blind harmonic instinct pierced the rind
  Of that slow life which made me straight and high,
And I became a harp for every wind,
    A voice for every sky;

When fierce autumnal gales began to blow,
  Roaring all day in concert, hoarse and deep;
And then made silent with my weight of snow,—
    A spectre on the steep;

Filled with a whispering gush, like that which flows
  Through organ-stops, when sank the sun's red disk
Beyond the city, and in blackness rose
    Temple and obelisk;

Or breathing soft, as one who sighs in prayer,
Mysterious sounds of portent and of might,
What time I felt the wandering waves of air
Pulsating through the night.

And thus for centuries my rhythmic chant
Rolled down the gorge or surged about the hill:
Gentle, or stern, or sad, or jubilant,
At every season's will.

No longer Memory whispers whence arose
The doom that tore me from my place of pride:
Whether the storms that load the peak with snows,
And start the mountain-slide,

Let fall a fiery bolt to smite my top,
Upwrenched my roots, and o'er the precipice
Hurled me, a dangling wreck, erelong to drop
Into the wild abyss;

Or whether hands of men, with scornful strength
And force from Nature's rugged armory lent,
Sawed through my heart and rolled my tumbling length
Sheer down the steep descent.

All sense departed, with the boughs I wore;
  And though I moved with mighty gales at strife,
A mast upon the seas, I sang no more,
    And music was my life.

Yet still that life awakens, brings again
  Its airy anthems, resonant and long,
Till Earth and Sky, transfigured, fill my brain
    With rhythmic sweeps of song.

Thence am I made a poet: thence are sprung
  Those motions of the soul, that sometimes reach
Beyond all grasp of Art, — for which the tongue
    Is ignorant of speech.

And if some wild, full-gathered harmony
  Roll its unbroken music through my line,
Believe there murmurs, faintly though it be,
    The Spirit of the Pine.

THE SOLDIER AND THE PARD.

A SECOND deluge! Well, — no matter: here,
At least, is better shelter than the lean,
Sharp-elbowed oaks — a dismal company! —
That stood around us in the mountain road
When that cursed axle broke: a roof of thatch,
A fire of withered boughs, and best of all,
This ruddy wine of Languedoc, that warms
One through and through, from heart to finger-ends.
No better quarters for a stormy night
A soldier, like myself, could ask; and since
The rough Cevennes refuse to let us forth,
Why, fellow-travellers, if so you will,
I 'll tell the story, cut so rudely short
When both fore-wheels broke from the diligence,
Stocked in the rut, and pitched us all together:

I said, we fought beside the Pyramids;

And somehow, from the glow of this good wine
And from the gloomy rain, that shuts one in
With his own self, — a sorry mate sometimes! —
The scene comes back like life. As then, I feel
The sun, and breathe the hot Egyptian air,
Hear Kleber, see the sabre of Dessaix
Flash at the column's front, and in the midst
Napoleon, upon his Barbary horse,
Calm, swarthy-browed, and wiser than the Sphinx
Whose porphyry lips guard Egypt's mystery.
Ha! what a rout! our cannon bellowed round
The Pyramids: the Mamelukes closed in,
And hand to hand like devils did we fight,
Rolled towards Aboukir in the smoke and sand.

For days we followed up the Nile. We pitched
Our tents in Memphis, pitched them on the site
Of Arsinoë, and beside the cliffs
Of Aboufayda. Then we came anon
On Kenneh, ere the sorely-frightened Bey
Had time to pack his harem: nay, we took
His camels, not his wives: and so, from day
To day, past wrecks of temples half submerged
In sandy inundation, till we saw
Old noseless Memnon sitting on the plain,
Both hands upon his knees, and in the east

Karnak's propylon and its pillared court.
The sphinxes wondered — such as had a face —
To see us stumbling down their avenues,
But we kept silent. One may whistle round
Your Roman temples here at Nismes, or dance
Upon the Pont du Gard ; — but, take my word,
Egyptian ruins are a serious thing :
You would not dare let fly a joke beside
The maimed colossi, though your very feet
Might catch between some mummied Pharaoh's ribs.

Dessaix had not enough of chasing Mamelukes,
And so we rummaged tomb and catacomb,
Clambered the hills and watched the Desert's rim
For sight of horse. One day, my company
(I was but ensign then) found far within
The sands, a two-days journey from the Nile,
A round oasis, like a jewel set.
It was a grove of date-trees, clustering close
About a tiny spring, whose overflow
Trickled beyond their shade a little space,
And the insatiate Desert licked it up.
The fiery ride, the glare of afternoon
Had burned our faces, so we stopped to feel
The coolness and the shadow, like a bath
Of pure ambrosial lymph, receive our limbs

And sweeten every sense. Drowsed by the soft,
Delicious greenness and repose, I crept
Into a balmy nest of yielding shrubs,
And floated off to slumber on a cloud
Of rapturous sensation.

When I woke,
So deep had been the oblivion of that sleep,
That Adam, when he woke in Paradise,
Was not more blank of knowledge; he had felt
As heedlessly, the silence and the shade;
As ignorantly had raised his eyes and seen —
As, for a moment, I — what then I saw
With terror, freezing limb and voice like death,
When the slow sense, supplying one lost link,
Ran with electric fleetness through the chain
And showed me what I was, — no miracle,
But lost and left alone amid the waste,
Fronting a deadly Pard, that kept great eyes
Fixed steadily on mine. I could not move:
My heart beat slow and hard: I sat and gazed,
With not a wink, upon those jasper orbs,
Noting the while, with horrible detail
Whereto my fascinated sight was bound,
Their tawny brilliance, and the spotted fell
That wrinkled round them, smoothly sloping back

And curving to the short and tufted ears.
I felt — and with a sort of fearful joy —
The beauty of the creature : 't was a pard,
Not such as one of those they show you caged
In Paris, — lean and scurvy beasts enough !
No : but a desert pard, superb and proud,
That would have died behind the villanous bars.

I think the creature had not looked on man,
For, as my brain grew cooler, I could see
Small sign of fierceness in her eyes, but chief,
Surprise and wonder. More and more entranced,
Her savage beauty warmed away the chill
Of death-like terror at my heart : I stared
With kindling admiration, and there came
A gradual softness o'er the flinty light
Within her eyes ; a shadow crept around
Their yellow disks, and something like a dawn
Of recognition of superior will,
Of brute affection, sympathy enslaved
By higher nature, then informed her face.
Thrilling in every nerve, I stretched my hand, —
She silent, moveless, — touched her velvet head,
And with a warm, sweet shiver in my blood,
Stroked down the ruffled hairs. She did not start ;
But, in a moment's lapse, drew up one paw

And moved a step, — another, — till her breath
Came hot upon my face. She stopped : she rolled
A deep-voiced note of pleasure and of love,
And gathering up her spotted length, lay down,
Her head upon my lap, and forward thrust
One heavy-moulded paw across my knees,
The glittering talons sheathing tenderly.
Thus we, in that oasis all alone,
Sat when the sun went down : the Pard and I,
Caressing and caressed : and more of love
And more of confidence between us came,
I grateful for my safety, she alive
With the dumb pleasure of companionship,
Which touched with instincts of humanity
Her brutish nature. When I slept, at last,
My arm was on her neck.

The morrow brought
No rupture of the bond between us twain.
The creature loved me ; she would bounding come,
Cat-like, to rub her great, smooth, yellow head
Against my knee, or with rough tongue would lick
The hand that stroked the velvet of her hide.
How beautiful she was ! how lithe and free
The undulating motions of her frame!
How shone, like isles of tawny gold, her spots,

Mapped on the creamy white! And when she walked,
No princess, with the crown about her brows,
Looked so superbly royal. Ah, my friends,
Smile as you may, but I would give this life
With its fantastic pleasures — ay, even that
One leads in Paris — to be back again
In the red Desert, with my splendid Pard.

That grove of date-trees was our home, our world,
A star of verdure in a sky of sand.
Without the feathery fringes of its shade
The naked Desert ran, its burning round
Sharp as a sword: the naked sky above,
Awful in its immensity, not shone
There only, where the sun supremely flamed,
But all its deep blue walls were penetrant
With dazzling light. God reigned in Heaven and Earth,
An Everlasting Presence, and his care
Fed us, alike his children. From the trees
That shook down pulpy dates, and from the spring,
The quiet author of that happy grove,
My wants were sated; and when midnight came,
Then would the Pard steal softly from my side,
Take the unmeasured sand with flying leaps
And vanish in the dusk, returning soon
With a gazelle's light carcass in her jaws.

So passed the days, and each the other taught
Our simple language. She would come at call
Of the pet name I gave her, bound and sport
When so I bade, and she could read my face
Through all its changing moods, with better skill
Than many a Christian comrade. Pard and beast,
Though you may say she was, she had a soul.

But Sin will find the way to Paradise.
Ere long, the sense of isolation fed
My mind with restless fancies. I began
To miss the life of camp, the march, the fight,
The soldier's emulation: youthful blood
Ran in my veins: the silence lost its charm,
And when the morning sunrise lighted up
The threshold of the Desert, I would gaze
With looks of bitter longing o'er the sand.
At last, I filled my soldier's sash with dates,
Drank deeply of the spring, and while the Pard
Roamed in the starlight for her forage, took
A westward course. The grove already lay
A dusky speck — no more — when through the night
Came the forsaken creature's eager cry.
Into a sandy pit I crept, and heard
Her bounding on my track, until she rolled
Down from the brink upon me. Then with cries

Of joy and of distress, the touching proof
Of the poor beast's affection, did she strive
To lift me — Pardon, friends! these foolish eyes
Must have their will: and had you seen her then,
In her mad gambols, as we homeward went,
Your hearts had softened too.

But I, possessed
By some vile devil of mistrust, became
More jealous and impatient. In my heart
I cursed the grove and with suspicions wronged
The noble Pard. She keeps me here, I thought,
Deceived with false caresses, as a cat
Toys with the trembling mouse she straight devours.
Will she so gently fawn about my feet,
When the gazelles are gone? Will she crunch dates,
And drink the spring, whose only drink is blood?
Am I to ruin flattered, and by whom? —
Not even a man, a wily beast of prey,
Thus did the Devil whisper in mine ear,
Till those black thoughts were rooted in my heart
And made me cruel. So it chanced one day,
That as I watched a flock of birds, that wheeled,
And dipped, and circled in the air, the Pard,
Moved by a freak of fond solicitude
To win my notice, closed her careful fangs

About my knee. Scarce knowing what I did,
In the blind impulse of suspicious fear,
I plunged, full home, my dagger in her neck.
God! could I but recall that blow! She loosed
Her hold, as softly as a lover quits
His mistress' lips, and with a single groan
Full of reproach and sorrow, sank and died.
What had I done! Sure never on this earth
Did sharper grief so base a deed requite.
Its murderous fury gone, my heart was racked
With pangs of wild contrition, spent itself
In cries and tears, the while I called on God
To curse me for my sin. There lay the Pard,
Her splendid eyes all film, her blazoned fell
Smirched with her blood; and I, her murderer,
Less than a beast, had thus repaid her love.

Ah, Friends, with all this guilty memory
My heart is sore: and little now remains
To tell you, but that afterwards — how long,
I never knew — our soldiers picked me up,
Wandering about the Desert, wild with grief
And sobbing like a child. My nerves have grown
Like steel, in many battles; I can step
Without a shudder through the heaps of slain;
But never, never, till the day I die,

Prevent a woman's weakness, when I think
Upon my desert Pard: and if a man
Deny this truth she taught me, to his face
I say he lies: a beast may have a soul.

ARIEL IN THE CLOVEN PINE.

Now the frosty stars are gone :
I have watched them, one by one,
Fading on the shores of Dawn.
Round and full the glorious sun
Walks with level step the spray,
Through his vestibule of Day,
While the wolves that late did howl
Slink to dens and coverts foul,
Guarded by the dęmon owl,
Who, last night, with mocking croon
Wheeled athwart the chilly moon,
And with eyes that blankly glared
On my direful torment stared.

The lark is flickering in the light ;
Still the nightingale doth sing ; —
All the isle, alive with Spring,
Lies, a jewel of delight

On the blue sea's heaving breast:
Not a breath from out the West,
But some balmy smell doth bring
From the sprouting myrtle buds,
Or from meadowy vales that lie
Like a green, inverted sky,
Which the yellow cowslip stars
And the bloomy almond woods,
Cloud-like, cross with roseate bars.
All is life that I can spy,
To the farthest sea and sky,
And my own the only pain
Within this ring of Tyrrhene main.

In the gnarled and cloven Pine
Where that hell-born hag did chain me,
All this orb of cloudless shine,
All this youth in Nature's veins
Tingling with the season's wine,
With a sharper torment pain me.
Pansies in soft April rains
Fill their stalks with honeyed sap
Drawn from Earth's prolific lap;
But the sluggish blood she brings
To the tough Pine's hundred rings,
Closer locks their cruel hold,

Closer draws the scaly bark
Round the crevice, damp and cold,
Where my useless wings I fold, —
Sealing me in iron dark.
By this coarse and alien state
Is my dainty essence wronged;
Finer senses that belonged
To my freedom, chafe at Fate,
Till the happier elves I hate,
Who in moonlight dances turn
Underneath the palmy fern,
Or in light and twinkling bands
Follow on with linkèd hands
To the Ocean's yellow sands.

Primrose-eyes each morning ope
In their cool, deep beds of grass;
Violets make the airs that pass
Telltales of their fragrant slope.
I can see them where they spring
Never brushed by fairy wing.
All those corners I can spy
In the island's solitude,
Where the dew is never dry,
Nor the miser bees intrude.

Cups of rarest hue are there,
Full of perfumed wine undrained, —
Mushroom banquets, ne'er profaned,
Canopied by maiden-hair.
Pearls I see upon the sands,
Never touched by other hands,
And the rainbow bubbles shine
On the ridged and frothy brine,
Tenantless of voyager
Till they burst in vacant air.
O the songs that sung might be
And the mazy dances woven,
Had that witch ne'er crossed the sea
And the Pine been never cloven !

Many years my direst pain
Has made the wave-rocked isle complain.
Winds, that from the Cyclades
Came, to ruffle with foul riot
Round its shore's enchanted quiet,
Bore my wailings on the seas ;
Sorrowing birds in Autumn went
Through the world with my lament.
Still the bitter fate is mine,
All delight unshared to see,

Smarting in the cloven Pine,
While I wait the tardy axe
Which, perchance, shall set me free
From the damned witch, Sycorax.

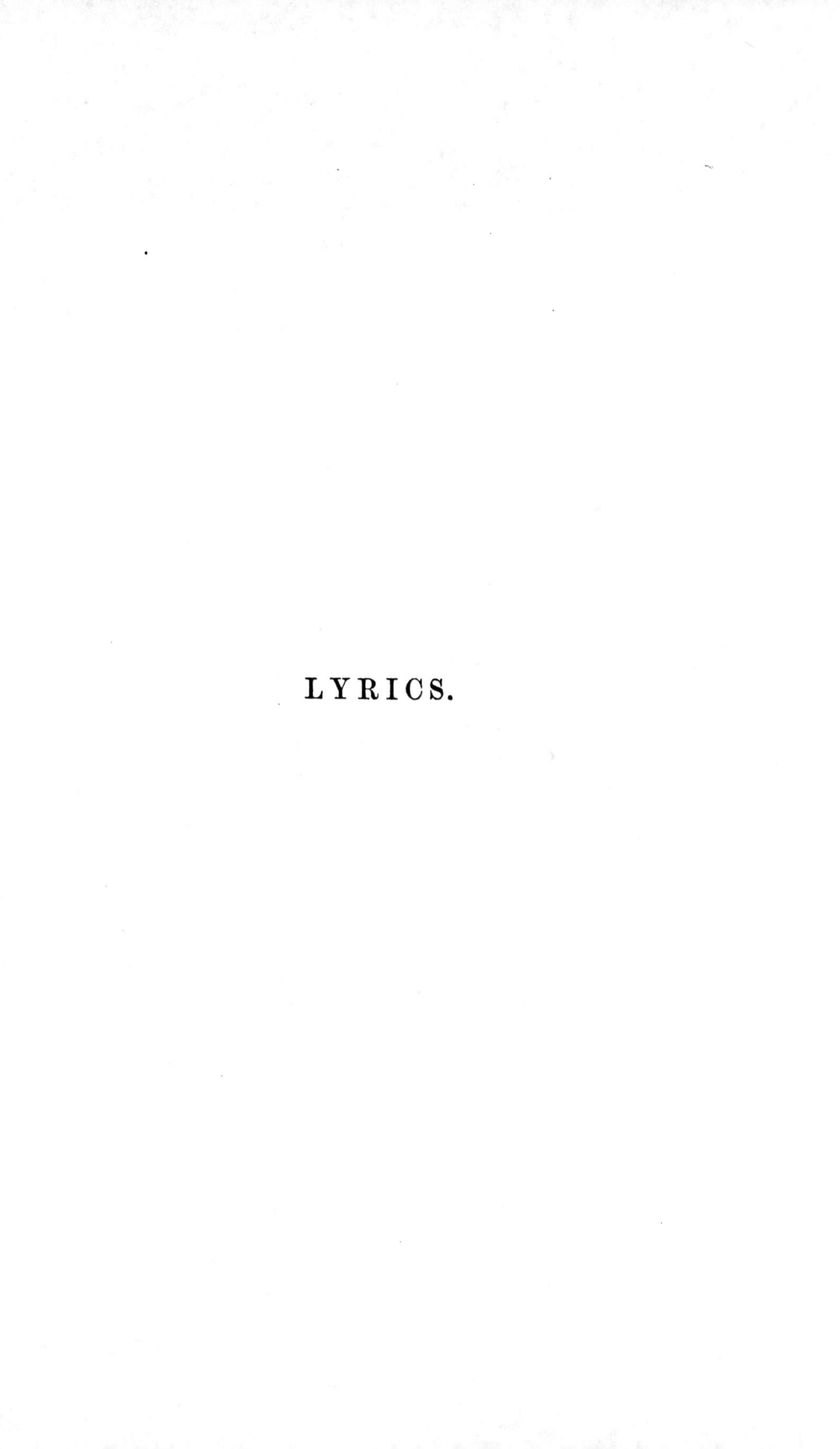

LYRICS.

THE HARP: AN ODE.

I.

When bleak winds through the Northern pines were
sweeping,
Some hero-skald, reclining on the sand,
Attuned it first, the chords harmonious keeping
With murmuring forest and with moaning strand:
And when, at night, the horns of mead foamed over,
And torches flared around the wassail board,
It breathed no song of maid nor sigh of lover,
It rang aloud the triumphs of the sword!
It mocked the thunders of the ice-ribbed ocean,
With clenched hands beating back the dragon's prow;
It gave Berserker arms their battle motion,
And swelled the red veins on the Viking's brow!

II.

No myrtle, plucked in dalliance, ever sheathed it,
    To melt the savage ardor of its flow;
The only gauds wherewith its lord enwreathed it,
    The lusty fir and Druid mistletoe.
Thus bound, it kept the old, accustomed cadence,
    Whether it pealed through slumberous ilex bowers
In stormy wooing of Byzantine maidens,
    Or shook Trinacria's languid lap of flowers;
Whether Genseric's conquering march it chanted,
    Till cloudy Atlas rang with Gothic staves,
Or where gray Calpè's pillared feet are planted,
    Died grandly out upon the unknown waves!

III.

Not unto Scania's bards alone belonging,
    The craft that loosed its tongues of changing sound,
For Ossian played, and ghosts of heroes, thronging,
    Leaned on their spears above the misty mound.
The Cambrian eagle, round his eyrie winging,
    Heard the wild chant through mountain-passes rolled,
When bearded throats chimed in with mighty singing,
    And monarchs listened, in their torques of gold:
Its dreary wail, blent with the sea-mews' clangor,
    Surged round the lonely keep of Penmaen-Mawr;
It pealed afar, in battle's glorious anger,
    Behind the banner of the Blazing Star!

IV.

The strings are silent: who shall dare to wake them,
  Though later deeds demand their living powers?
Silent in other lands, what hand shall make them
  Leap as of old, to shape the songs of ours?
Here, while the sapless bulk of Europe moulders,
  Springs the rich blood to hero-veins unsealed,—
Source of that Will, that on its fearless shoulders
  Would bear the world's fate lightly as a shield:
Here moves a larger life, to grander measures
  Beneath our sky and through our forests rung;
Why sleeps the harp, forgetful of its treasures,—
  Buried in songs, that never yet were sung?

V.

Great, solemn songs, that with majestic sounding
  Should swell the Nation's heart, from sea to sea;
Informed with power, with earnest hope abounding,
  And prophecies of triumph yet to be!
Songs, by the wild wind for a thousand ages
  Hummed o'er our central prairies, vast and lone;
Glassed by the Northern lakes in crystal pages,
  And carved by hills on pinnacles of stone:
Songs chanted now, where undiscovered fountains
  Make in the wilderness their babbling home,
And through the deep-hewn cañons of the mountains
  Plunge the cold rivers in perpetual foam!

VI.

Sung but by these: our forests have no voices;
  Rapt with no loftier strain our rivers roll;
Far in the sky, no song-crowned peak rejoices
  In sounds that give the silent air a soul.
Wake, mighty Harp! and thrill the shores that hearken
  For the first peal of thine immortal rhyme:
Call from the shadows that begin to darken
  The beaming forms of our heroic time:
Sing us of deeds, that on thy strings outsoaring
  The ancient soul they glorified so long,
Shall win the world to hear thy grand restoring,
  And own thy latest thy sublimest song!

MANUELA.

A BALLAD OF CALIFORNIA.

From the doorway, Manuela, in the sheeny April morn,
Southward looks, along the valley, over leagues of gleaming corn;
Where the mountain's misty rampart like the wall of Eden towers,
And the isles of oak are sleeping on a painted sea of flowers.

All the air is full of music, for the winter rains are o'er,
And the noisy magpies chatter from the budding sycamore;
Blithely frisk unnumbered squirrels, over all the grassy slope;
Where the airy summits brighten, nimbly leaps the antelope.

Gentle eyes of Manuela! tell me wherefore do ye
rest
On the oak's enchanted islands and the flowery ocean's
breast?
Tell me wherefore, down the valley, ye have traced
the highway's mark
Far beyond the belts of timber, to the mountain-shad-
ows dark?

Ah, the fragrant bay may blossom and the sprouting
verdure shine
With the tears of amber dropping from the tassels of
the pine,
And the morning's breath of balsam lightly brush her
sunny cheek, —
Little recketh Manuela of the tales of Spring they
speak.

When the Summer's burning solstice on the mountain-
harvests glowed,
She had watched a gallant horseman riding down the
valley road;
Many times she saw him turning, looking back with
parting thrills,
Till amid her tears she lost him, in the shadow of the
hills.

Ere the cloudless moons were over, he had passed the
Desert's sand,
Crossed the rushing Colorado and the wild Apachè
Land,
And his laden mules were driven, when the time of rains
began,
With the traders of Chihuahua, to the Fair of San
Juan.

Therefore watches Manuela, — therefore lightly doth
she start,
When the sound of distant footsteps seems the beating
of her heart;
Not a wind the green oak rustles or the redwood
branches stirs,
But she hears the silver jingle of his ringing bit and
spurs.

Often, out the hazy distance, come the horsemen, day
by day,
But they come not as Bernardo, — she can see it, far
away;
Well she knows the airy gallop of his mettled alazàn,
Light as any antelope upon the Hills of Gavilàn.

She would know him 'mid a thousand, by his free and gallant air;
By the featly-knit sarápè, such as wealthy traders wear;
By his broidered calzoneros and his saddle, gaily spread,
With its cantle rimmed with silver, and its horn a lion's head.

None like him the light riáta on the maddened bull can throw;
None amid the mountain-cañons, track like him the stealthy doe;
And at all the Mission festals, few indeed the revellers are
Who can dance with him the jota, touch with him the gay guitar.

He has said to Manuela, and the echoes linger still
In the cloisters of her bosom, with a secret, tender thrill,
When the bay again has blossomed, and the valley stands in corn,
Shall the bells of Santa Clara usher in the wedding morn.

He has pictured the procession, all in holiday attire,
And the laugh and look of gladness, when they see the distant spire;
Then their love shall kindle newly, and the world be doubly fair,
In the cool, delicious crystal of the summer morning air.

Tender eyes of Manuela! what has dimmed your lustrous beam?
'T is a tear that falls to glitter on the casket of her dream.
Ah, the eye of Love must brighten, if its watches would be true,
For the star is falsely mirrored in the rose's drop of dew!

But her eager eyes rekindle and her breathless bosom stills,
As she sees a horseman moving in the shadow of the hills:
Now in love and fond thanksgiving they may loose their pearly tides, —
'T is the alazàn that gallops, 't is Bernardo's self that rides!

TAURUS.

I.

THE Scorpion's stars crawl down behind the sun,
  And when he drops below the verge of day,
The glittering fangs, their fervid courses run,
  Cling to his skirts and follow him away.
Then, ere the heels of flying Capricorn
  Have touched the western mountain's fading rim,
I mark, stern Taurus, through the twilight gray
      The glinting of thy horn,
  And sullen front uprising large and dim,
Bent to the starry hunter's sword, at bay.

II.

Thy hoofs, unwilling, climb the sphery vault;
  Thy red eye trembles with an angry glare,
When the hounds follow, and in fierce assault
  Bay through the fringes of the lion's hair.
The stars that once were mortal in their love,
  And by their love are made immortal now,
Cluster like golden bees upon thy mane,
    When thou, possessed with Jove,
  Bore sweet Europa's garlands on thy brow
And stole her from the green Sicilian plain.

III.

Type of the stubborn force that will not bend
  To loftier art, — soul of defiant breath
That blindly stands and battles to the end,
  Nerving resistance with the throes of death, —
Majestic Taurus! when thy wrathful eye
  Flamed brightest, and thy hoofs a moment stayed
Their march at Night's meridian, I was born:
    But in the western sky,
  Like sweet Europa, Love's fair star delayed,
To hang her garland on thy silver horn.

IV.

Thou giv'st that temper of enduring mould,
That slights the wayward bent of Destiny, —
Such as sent forth the shaggy Jarls of old
To launch their dragons on the unknown sea:
Such as kept strong the sinews of the sword,
The proud, hot blood of battle, — welcome made
The headsman's axe, the rack, the martyr-fire,
The ignominious cord,
When but to yield, had pomps and honors laid
On heads that moulder in ignoble mire.

V.

Night is the summer when the soul grows ripe
With Life's full harvest: of her myriad suns,
Thou dost not gild the quiet herdsman's pipe
Nor royal state, that royal action shuns.
But in the noontide of thy ruddy stars
Thrive strength, and daring, and the blood whence springs
The Heraclidean seed of heroes: then
Were sundered Gaza's bars;
Then, 'mid the smitten Hydra's loosened rings,
His slayer rested, in the Lernean fen.

VI.

Thou sway'st the heart's red tides, until they bear
  The kindled spirit on their mounting wave,
To Glory's flood-mark ; in thy steadfast glare
  Age thaws his ice, and thrills beside the grave.
Not Bacchus, by his span of panthers borne,
  And flushed with triumph of the purple vine,
Can give his sons so fierce a joy as thou,
    When, filled with pride and scorn,
  Thou mak'st relentless anger seem divine,
And all Jove's terror clothes a mortal brow.

VII.

Thine is the subtle element that turns
  To fearless act the impulse of the hour, —
The secret fire, whose flash electric burns
  To every source of passion and of power.
Therefore I hail thee, on thy glittering track :
  Therefore I watch thee, when the night grows dark,
Slow-rising, front Orion's sword along
    The starry zodiac,
  And from thy mystic beam demand a spark
To warm my soul with more heroic song.

THE SUMMER CAMP.

[CALIFORNIA]

Here slacken rein; here let the dusty mules
Unsaddled graze! The shadows of the oaks
Are on our brows, and through their knotted boles
We see the blue round of the boundless plain
Vanish in glimmering heat: these aged oaks,
The island speck that beckoned us afar
Over the burning level, — as we came,
Spreading to shore and cape, and bays that ran
To leafy headlands, balanced on the haze,
Faint and receding as a cloud of air.

The mules may roam unsaddled: we will lie
Beneath the mighty trees, whose shade, like dew
Poured from the urns of Twilight, dries the sweat
Of sunburnt brows, and on the heavy lid
And heated eyeball sheds a balm, than sleep

Far sweeter. We have done with travel, — we
Are weary now, who never dreamed of Rest,
For until now did never Rest unbar
Her palace-doors, nor until now our ears
The silence drink, beyond all melodies
Of all imagined sound, that wraps her realm.
Here, where the desolating centuries
Have left no mark; where noises never came
From the far world of battle and of toil;
Where God looks down and sends no thunderbolt
To smite a human wrong, for all is good,
She finds a refuge. We will dwell with her.

No more of travel, where the flaming sword
Of the great sun divides the heavens; no more
Of climbing over jutty steeps that swim
In driving sea-mist, where the stunted tree
Slants inland, mimicking the stress of winds
When wind is none; of plain and steaming marsh
Where the dry bulrush crackles in the heat;
Of camps by starlight in the columned vault
Of sycamores, and the red, dancing fires
That build a leafy arch, efface and build,
And sink at last, to let the stars peep through;
Of cañons grown with pine and folded deep
In golden mountain-sides; of airy sweeps

Of mighty landscape, lying all alone
Like some deserted world. They tempt no more.
It is enough that such things were: too blest,
O comrades mine, to lie in Summer's arms,
Lodged in her Camp of Rest, we will not dream
That they may vex us more.

The sun goes down:
The dun mules wander idly: motionless
Beneath the stars, the heavy foliage lifts
Its rich, round masses, silent as a cloud
That sleeps at mid-day on a mountain peak.
All through the long, delicious night no stir
Is in the leaves; spangled with broken gleams,
Before the pining Moon — that fain would drop
Into the lap of this deep quiet — swerve
Eastward the shadows: Day comes on again.
Where is the life we led? Whither hath fled
The turbulent stream that brought us hither? How,
So full of sound, so lately dancing down
The mountains, turbid, fretted into foam, —
How has it slipped, with scarce a gurgling coil,
Into this calm transparence, noise or wind
Hath ruffled never? Ages past, perchance,
Such wild turmoil was ours, or did some Dream
Malign, that last night nestled in the oak,

Whisper our ears, when not a star could see?
Give o'er the fruitless doubt: we will not waste
One thought of rest, nor spill one radiant drop
From the full goblet of this summer balm.

Day after day the mellow sun slides o'er,
Night after night the mellow moon. The clouds
Are laid, enchanted: soft and bare, the heavens
Fold to their breast the dozing Earth, that lies
In languor of deep bliss. At times, a breath,
Remnant of gales far off, forgotten now,
Tinkles the never-fading leaves, then drops
Affrighted into silence. Near a slough
Of dark, still water, in the early morn
The shy coyotas prowl, or trooping elk
From the close covert of the bulrush-fields
Their dewy antlers toss: nor other sight,
Save when the falcon, poised on wheeling wings,
His bright eye on the burrowing coney, cuts
His arrowy plunge. Along the distant trail,
Dim with the heat, sometimes the miners go
Bearded and rough, the swart Sonorians drive
Their laden asses, or vaqueros whirl
The lasso's coil and carol many a song
Native to Spanish hills. As when we lie
On the soft brink of Sleep, not pillowed quite

To blest forgetfulness, some dim array
Of masking forms in long procession comes,
A sweet disturbance to the poppied sense,
That will not cease, but gently holds it back
From slumber's haven, so their figures pass,
With such disturbance cloud the blessed calm
And hold our beings, ready to slip forth
O'er unmolested seas, still-rocking near
The coasts of Action.

Other dreams are ours,
Of shocks that were, or seemed ; whereof our souls
Feel the subsiding lapse, as feels the sand
Of tropic island-shores the dying pulse
Of storms that racked the Northern sea. My Soul,
I do believe that thou hast toiled and striven,
And hoped and suffered wrong. I do believe
Great aims were thine, deep loves and fiery hates,
And though I may have lain a thousand years
Beneath these Oaks, the baffled trust of Youth,
Thy first keen sorrow, brings a gentle pang
To temper joy. Nor will the joy I drank
To wild intoxication, quit my heart :
It was no dream that still has power to droop
The soft-suffusing lid, and lift desire
Beyond this rapt repose. No dream, dear love !
For thou art with me in our Camp of Peace.

O Friend, whose history is writ in deeds
That make your life a marvel, come no gleams
Of past adventure, echoes of old storms,
And Battle's tingling hum of flying shot,
To touch your easy blood and tempt you o'er
The round of yon blue plain? Or have they lost,
Heroic days, the virtue which the heart
That did their hest rejoicing, proved so high?
Back through the long, long cycles of our rest
Your memory travels: through this hush you hear
The Gila's dashing, feel the yawning jaws
Of black volcanic gorges close you in
On waste and awful tracts of wilderness,
Which other than the eagle's cry, or bleat
Of mountain-goat, hear not: the scorching sand
Eddies around the tracks your fainting mules
Leave in the Desert: thorn and cactus pierce
Your bleeding limbs, and stiff with raging thirst
Your tongue forgets its office. Leave untried
That cruel trail, and leave the wintry hills
And leave the tossing sea! The Summer here
Builds us a tent of everlasting calm.

How shall we wholly sink our lives in thee,
Thrice-blessed Deep? O many-natured Soul,
Chameleon-like, that, steeped in every phase

Of wide existence, tak'st the hue of each,
Here with the silent Oaks and azure Air
Incorporate grow! Here loosen one by one
Thy vexing memories, burdens of the Past,
Till all unrest be laid, and strong Desire
Sleeps on his nerveless arm. Content to find
In liberal Peace thy being's high result
And crown of aspiration, gather all
The dreams of sense, the reachings of the mind
For ampler issues and dominion vain,
To fold them on her bosom, happier there
Than in exultant action: as a child
Forgets his meadow butterflies and flowers,
Upon his mother's breast.

It may not be.
Not in this Camp, in these enchanted Trees,
But in ourselves, must lodge the calm we seek,
Ere we can fix it here. We cannot take
From outward nature power to snap the curse
Which clothed our birth; and though 't were easier
This hour to die, than yield the blessed cup
Wherefrom our hearts divinest comfort draw,
It clothes us yet, and yet shall drive us forth
To breast the world. Then come: we will not bide
To tempt a ruin to this paradise,

Fulfilling Destiny. A mighty wind
Would gather on the plain, a cloud arise
To blot the sky, with thunder in its heart,
And the black column of the whirlwind spin
Out of the cloud, straight downward to this grove,
Take by their heads the shuddering trees, and wrench
With fearful clamor, limb from limb, till Rest
Should flee for ever. Rather set at once
Our faces toward the noisy world again,
And gird our loins for action. Let us go !

MOAN, ye wild winds! around the pane,
And fall, thou drear December rain!
Fill with your gusts the sullen day,
Tear the last clinging leaves away!
Reckless as yonder naked tree,
No blast of yours can trouble me.

Give me your chill and wild embrace,
And pour your baptism on my face;
Sound in mine ears the airy moan
That sweeps in desolate monotone,
Where on the unsheltered hill-top beat
The marches of your homeless feet!

Moan on, ye winds! and pour, thou rain!
Your stormy sobs and tears are vain,
If shed for her, whose fading eyes
Will open soon on Paradise:
The eye of Heaven shall blinded be,
Or ere ye cease, if shed for me.

SERAPION.

Come hither, Child! thou silent, shy
Young creature of the glorious eye!
Though never yet by ruder air
Than father's kiss or mother's prayer
Were stirred the tendrils of thy hair,
The sadness of a soul that stands
Withdrawn from Childhood's frolic bands,
A stranger in the land, I trace
Upon thy brow's cherubic grace,
The tender pleading of thy face,
Where other stars than Joy and Hope
Have cast thy being's horoscope.

For thee, the threshold of the world
Is yet with morning dews impearled;
The nameless radiance of Birth
Embathes thy atmosphere of Earth,

And, like a finer sunshine, swims
Round every motion of thy limbs:
The sweet, sad wonder and surprise
Of waking, glimmers in thine eyes,
And wiser instinct, purer sense,
And gleams of rare intelligence
Betray the converse held by thee
In the angelic family.

Come hither, Boy! For while I press
Thy lip's confiding tenderness,
Less broad and dark the spaces be
Which Life has set 'twixt thee and me.
Thy soul's white feet shall soon depart
On paths I walked with eager heart;
God give thee, in His kindly grace,
A brighter road, a loftier place!
I see thy generous nature flow
In boundless trust, to friend and foe,
And leap, despite of shocks and harms,
To clasp the world in loving arms.
I see that glorious circle shrink
Back to thy feet, at Manhood's brink,
Narrowed to one, one image fair,
And all its splendor gathered there.
The shackles of experience then
Sit lightly as on meaner men:

In flinty paths thy feet may bleed,
Thorns pierce thy flesh, thou shalt not heed,
Till when, all panting from the task,
Thine arms outspread their right shall ask,
Thine arms outspread that right shall fly,
The star shall burst, the splendor die!
Go, with thy happier brothers play,
As heedless and as wild as they;
Seek not so soon thy separate way,
Thou lamb in Childhood's field astray!

Whence camest thou? what angel bore
Thee past so many a fairer shore
Of guarding love and guidance mild,
To drop thee on this barren wild?
Thy soul is lonely as a star
When all its fellows muffled are, —
A single star, whose light appears
To glimmer through subduing tears.
The father who begat thee sees
In thee no deeper mysteries
Than load his heavy leger's page,
And swell for him thy heritage.
A hard, cold man, of punctual face,
Renowned in Credit's holy-place,
Whose very wrinkles seem arrayed
In cunning hieroglyphs of trade, —

Whose gravest thought but just unlocks
The problems of uncertain stocks, —
Whose farthest flights of hope extend
From dividend to dividend.
Thy mother, — but a mother's name
Too sacred is, too sweet for blame.
No doubt she loves thee, — loves the shy,
Strange beauty of thy glorious eye;
Loves the soft mouth, whose drooping line
Is silent music; loves to twine
Thy silky hair in ringlets trim;
To watch thy lightsome play of limb;
But, God forgive me! I, who find
The soul within that beauty shrined,
I love thee more, I know thy worth
Better, than she who gave thee birth.

Are they thy keepers? They would thrust
The priceless jewel in the dust;
Would tarnish in their careless hold
The vessel of celestial gold.
Who gave them thee? What fortune lent
Their hands the delicate instrument,
Which finer hands might teach to hymn
The harmonies of Seraphim,
Which they shall make discordant soon,
The sweet bells jangled, out of tune?

Mine eyes are dim: I cannot see
The purposes of Destiny,
But than my love Heaven could not shine
More lovingly, if thou wert mine!
Yes, Child! even now, there cannot be
Such boundless tenderness for thee.
Rest thou securely on my heart:
Give me thy trust: *my* child thou art,
And I shall lead thee through the years
To Hopes and Passions, Loves and Fears,
Till, following up Life's endless plan,
A strong and self-dependent Man,
I see thee stand and strive with men:
Thy Father now, thy Brother then.

THE ODALISQUE.

In marble shells the fountain splashes;
  Its falling spray is turned to stars,
When some light wind its pinion dashes
  Against thy gilded lattice-bars.
Around the shafts, in breathing cluster,
  The roses of Damascus run,
And through the summer's moons of lustre
  The tulip's goblet drinks the sun.

The day, through shadowy arches fainting,
  Reveals the garden's burst of bloom,
With lights of shifting iris painting
  The jasper pavement of thy room:
Enroofed with palm and laurel bowers,
  Thou seest, beyond, the cool kiosk,
And far away, the pencilled towers
  That shoot from many a stately mosque.

Thou hast no world beyond the chamber
  Whose inlaid marbles mock the flowers,
Where burns thy lord's chibouk of amber,
  To charm the languid evening hours.
There sounds, for thee, the fond lute's yearning
  Through all enchanted tales of old,
And spicy cressets, dimly burning,
  Swing on their chains of Persian gold.

No more, in half-remembered vision,
  Thy distant childhood comes to view;
That star-like world of shapes Elysian
  Has faded from thy morning's blue:
The eastern winds that cross the Taurus
  Have now no voice of home beyond,
Where light waves foam in endless chorus
  Against the walls of Trebizond.

For thee the Past may never reckon
  Its hoard of saddening memories o'er,
Nor shapes from out the Future beckon
  To joys that only live in store.
Thy life is in the gorgeous Present,
  An orient summer, warm and bright;—
No gleam of beauty evanescent,
  But one long time of deep delight.

ADRIFT.

We sailed on a tranquil sea,
  A moon ago — no more,
And the god that steered securely neared
  The haven and the shore.

There was no reef below,
  No cloud above :
The only gale that swelled our sail
  To the blissful harbor drove.

Where now the mirrored keel,
  The splendor overhead ?
Billows dark have whelmed the bark
  And the faithless sun is dead.

In the darkness and the dread
  I drift alone :
Heaven hangs black on the dismal track
  Of the waves unknown.

Heaven hangs black and cold
  And the shores are far and dim ;
On a shattered plank of the ship that sank
  I feebly swim.

And the shores recede afar
  Behind the waves unknown ; —
On the sea no sail, in the sky no star :
God, in whose hand Thy creatures are,
  How shall I drift alone ?

THE PINE FOREST OF MONTEREY.

What point of Time, unchronicled, and dim
As yon gray mist that canopies your heads,
Took from the greedy wave and gave the sun
Your dwelling-place, ye gaunt and hoary Pines?
When, from the barren bosoms of the hills,
With scanty nurture, did ye slowly climb,
Of these remote and latest-fashioned shores
The first-born forest? Titans gnarled and rough,
Such as from out subsiding Chaos grew
To clothe the cold loins of the savage earth,
What fresh commixture of the elements,
What earliest thrill of life, the stubborn soil
Slow-mastering, engendered ye to give
The hills a mantle and the wind a voice?
Along the shore ye lift your rugged arms,
Blackened with many fires, and with hoarse chant—
Unlike the fibrous lute your co-mates touch
In elder regions — fill the awful stops

Between the crashing cataracts of the surf.
Have ye no tongue, in all your sea of sound,
To syllable the secret, — no still voice
To give your airy myths a shadowy form,
And make us of lost centuries of lore
The rich inheritors?

The sea-winds pluck
Your mossy beards, and gathering as they sweep,
Vex your high heads, and with your sinewy arms
Grapple and toil in vain. A deeper roar,
Sullen and cold, and rousing into spells
Of stormy volume, is your sole reply.
Anchored in firm-set rock, ye ride the blast
And from the promontory's utmost verge
Make signal o'er the waters. So ye stood,
When, like a star, behind the lonely sea,
Far shone the white speck of Grijalva's sail;
And when, through driving fog, the breaker's sound
Frighted Otondo's men, your spicy breath
Played as in welcome round their rusty helms,
And backward from its staff shook out the folds
Of Spain's emblazoned banner.

Ancient Pines,
Ye bear no record of the years of man.

Spring is your sole historian, — Spring, that paints
These savage shores with hues of Paradise ;
That tricks with glowing green your branches out,
And through your lonely, far cañadas pours
Her floods of bloom, rivers of opal dye
That wander down to lakes and widening seas
Of blossom and of fragrance, — laughing Spring,
That with her wanton blood refills your veins,
And weds ye to your juicy youth again
With a new ring, the while your rifted bark
Drops odorous tears. Your knotty fibres yield
To the light touch of her unfailing pen,
As freely as the lupin's violet cup.
Ye keep, close-locked, the memories of her stay,
As in their shells the avelonès keep
Morn's rosy flush and moonlight's pearly glow.
The wild northwest, that from Alaska sweeps,
To drown Point Lobos with the icy scud
And white sea-foam, may rend your boughs and leave
Their blasted antlers tossing in the gale ;
Your steadfast hearts are mailed against the shock,
And on their annual tablets naught inscribe
Of such rude visitation. Ye are still
The simple children of a guiltless soil,
And in your natures show the sturdy grain
That passion cannot jar, nor force relax,

Nor aught but sweet and kindly airs compel
To gentler mood. No disappointed heart
Has sighed its bitterness beneath your shade;
No angry spirit ever came to make
Your silence its confessional; no voice,
Grown harsh in Crime's great market-place, the world,
Tainted with blasphemy your evening hush
And aromatic air. The deer alone,—
The ambushed hunter that brings down the deer,—
The fisher wandering on the misty shore
To watch sea-lions wallow in the flood,—
The shout, the sound of hoofs that chase and fly,
When swift vaqueros, dashing through the herds,
Ride down the angry bull,—perchance, the song
Some Indian heired of long-forgotten sires,—
Disturb your solemn chorus.

Stately Pines,
But few more years around the promontory
Your chant will meet the thunders of the sea.
No more, a barrier to the encroaching sand,
Against the surf ye'll stretch defiant arm,
Though with its onset and besieging shock
Your firm knees tremble. Never more the wind
Shall pipe shrill music through your mossy beards,
Nor sunset's yellow blaze athwart your heads

Crown all the hills with gold. Your race is past:
The mystic cycle, whose unnoted birth
Coeval was with yours, has run its sands,
And other footsteps from these changing shores
Frighten its haunting Spirit. Men will come
To vex your quiet with the din of toil;
The smoky volumes of the forge will stain
This pure, sweet air; loud keels will ride the sea,
Dashing its glittering sapphire into foam;
Through all her green cañadas Spring will seek
Her lavish blooms in vain, and clasping ye,
O mournful Pines, within her glowing arms,
Will weep soft rains to find ye fallen low.
Fall, therefore, yielding to the fiat! Fall,
Ere the maturing soil, whose first dull life
Fed your belated germs, be rent and seamed!
Fall, like the chiefs ye sheltered, stern, unbent,
Your gray beards hiding memorable scars!
The winds will mourn ye, and the barren hills
Whose breast ye clothed; and when the pauses come
Between the crashing cataracts of the surf,
A funeral silence, terrible, profound,
Will make sad answer to the listening sea.

SORROWFUL MUSIC.

GIVE me music, or I die;
Music, wherein Sorrow's cry
Is a sweet, aerial sigh, —
Where Despair is harmony.

Give me music, such as winds
To the ambushed grief, and finds
Clews of soft-enticing sound,
Notes that soothe and cannot wound,
Leading with a tender care
Outward into brighter air:
Music which, with welcome pain,
Melted from the master's brain,
When his sorrow, freed from smart,
Laid its head upon his heart,
And the measure, broken, slow, —
Shed with tears in mingled flow, —

All its mighty secret spake
And it slept : it will not wake.

Give me music, sad and strong,
Drawn from deeper founts than Song ;
More impassioned, full, and free
Than the Poet's numbers be :
Music which can master thee,
Stern enchantress, Memory !
Piercing through the darkened stress
Of thy spells of weariness,
As the summer lightnings play
Through a cloud's edge, far away.

Give me music, such as springs
When an angel droops his wings,
Pausing in mid-heaven, with eyes
Soft with dew of Paradise,
Hearing Love's thanksgiving rise
Out of hearts, whose living bloom
Hides the desolating tomb.

Give me music, I am dumb ;
Choked with tears that never come.
Give me music ; sigh or word
Such a sorrow never stirred,—

109

Sorrow that with blinding pain
Lies like fire on heart and brain.
Earth and Heaven bring no relief;
I am dumb; this weight of grief
Locks my lips; I cannot cry:
Give me music, or I die.

THE TULIP-TREE.

Now my blood, with long-forgotten fleetness,
  Bounds again to Boyhood's blithest tune,
While I drink a life of brimming sweetness
  From the glory of the breezy June.
Far above, the fields of ether brighten ;
  Forest leaves are twinkling in their glee ;
And the daisy's snows around me whiten,
  Drifted down the sloping lea !

On the hills he standeth as a tower,
  Shining in the morn, — the Tulip-Tree !
On his rounded turrets beats the shower,
  While his emerald flags are flapping free :
But when Summer, 'mid her harvests standing,
  Pours to him the sun's unmingled wine,
O'er his branches, all at once expanding,
  How the starry blossoms shine !

Through the glossy leaves they burn, unfolded,
Like the fiery-breasted oriole, —
Filled with sweetness, as a joy new moulded
Into being by a poet's soul!
Violet hills, against the sunrise lying,
See them kindle when the stars grow pale,
And their lips, unclosed in balmy sighing,
Sweeten all the morning gale.

Then all day, in every opening chalice,
Drains their honey-drops the revelling bee,
Till the dove-winged Sleep makes thee her palace,
Filled with song-like murmurs, Tulip-Tree!
In thine arms are rocked the dreams enchanted
Which in Childhood's heart their dwelling made;
Dreams, whose glory to my brain is granted,
When I lie amid thy shade.

Now, while Earth's full heart is throbbing over
With its wealth of light and life and joy,
Who can feel how later years shall cover
With their blight, the visions of the boy?
Who can see the shadows downward darken,
While the splendid morning bids aspire,
Or the turf upon his coffin hearken,
When his pulses leap with fire!

Wind of June, that sweep'st the rolling meadow,
  Thou shalt wail in branches rough and bare,
While the tree, o'erhung with storm and shadow,
  Writhes and creaks amid the gusty air.
All his leaves, like shields of fairies scattered,
  Then shall drop before the North-wind's spears,
And his limbs, by hail and tempest battered,
  Feel the weight of wintry years.

Yet, why cloud the rapture and the glory
  Of the Beautiful, bequeathed us now?
Why relinquish all the Summer's story,
  Calling up the bleak autumnal bough?
Let thy blossoms in the morning brighten,
  Happy heart, as doth the Tulip-Tree,
While the daisy's snows around us whiten,
  Drifted down the sloping lea!

AUTUMNAL VESPERS.

THE clarion Wind, that blew so loud at morn,
Whirling a thousand leaves from every bough
Of the purple woods, has not a whisper now;
Hushed on the uplands is the huntsman's horn,
And huskers whistling round the tented corn:
The snug warm cricket lets his clock run down,
Scared by the chill, sad hour, that makes forlorn
The Autumn's gold and brown.

The light is dying out on field and wold;
The life is dying in the leaves and grass.
The World's last breath no longer dims the glass
Of waning sunset, yellow, pale, and cold.
His genial pulse, which Summer made so bold,
Has ceased. Haste, Night, and spread thy decent pall!
The silent, stiffening Frost makes havoc: fold
The darkness over all!

The light is dying out o'er all the land,
And in my heart the light is dying. She,
My life's best life, is fading silently
From Earth, from me, and from the dreams we planned
Since first Love led us with his beaming hand
From hope to hope, yet kept his crown in store.
The light is dying out o'er all the land:
To me it comes no more.

The blossom of my heart, she shrinks away,
Stricken with deadly blight: more wan and weak
Her love replies in blanching lip and cheek,
And gentler in her dear eyes, day by day.
God, in Thy mercy bid the arm delay,
Which through her being smites to dust my own!
Thou gav'st the seed thy sun and showers: why slay
The blossoms yet unblown?

In vain, — in vain! God will not bid the Spring
Replace with sudden green the Autumn's gold;
And as the night-mists, gathering damp and cold,
Strike up the vales where water-courses sing,
Death's mist shall strike along her veins, and cling
Thenceforth for ever round her glorious frame:
For all her radiant presence, May shall bring
A memory and a name.

What know the woods, that soon shall be so stark,
    What know the barren fields, the songless air,
    Locked in benumbing cold, of blooms more fair
In mornings ushered by the April lark?
Weak solace this, which Grief will never hark;
    Blind as a bud in stiff December's mail,
To lift her look beyond the frozen dark
        No memory can avail.

I never knew the autumnal eves could wear,
    With all their pomp, so drear a hue of Death;
    I never knew their still and solemn breath
Could rob the breaking heart of strength to bear,
Feeding the blank submission of despair.
    Yet, peace, sad soul! reproach and pity shine
Suffused through starry tears: bend thou in prayer,
        Rebuked by Love divine.

Our life is scarce the twinkle of a star
    In God's eternal day. Obscure and dim
    With mortal clouds, it yet may beam for Him,
And darkened here, shine fair to spheres afar.
I will be patient, lest my sorrow bar
    His grace and blessing, and I fall supine:
In my own hands my want and weakness are,—
        My strength, O God! in Thine.

ODE TO SHELLEY.

I.

Why art thou dead? Upon the hills once more
  The golden mist of waning Autumn lies;
The slow-pulsed billows wash along the shore
  And phantom isles are floating in the skies.
They wait for thee: a spirit in the sand
  Hushes, expectant for thy coming tread;
The light wind pants to lift thy trembling hair;
      Inward, the silent land
  Lies with its mournful woods;—why art thou dead,
When Earth demands that thou shalt call her fair?

II.

Why art thou dead? I too demand thy song,
  To speak the language yet denied to mine,
Twin-doomed with thee, to feel the scorn of Wrong,
  To worship Beauty as a thing divine!
Thou art afar: wilt thou not soon return
  To tell me that which thou hast never told?
To clasp my throbbing hand, and, by the shore
      Or dewy mountain-fern,
  Pour out thy heart as to a friend of old,
Touched with a twilight sadness? Nevermore.

III.

I could have told thee all the sylvan joy
  Of trackless woods; the meadows far apart,
Within whose fragrant grass, a lonely boy,
  I thought of God; the trumpet at my heart,
When on bleak mountains roared the midnight storm
  And I was bathed in lightning, broad and grand:
O, more than all, with low and sacred breath
      And forehead flushing warm,
  I would have led thee through the summer land
Of early Love, and past my dreams of Death!

IV.

In thee, Immortal Brother! had I found
  That Voice of Earth, that flies my feebler lines:
The awful speech of Rome's sepulchral ground;
  The dusky hymn of Vallombrosa's pines!
From thee, the noise of Ocean would have taken
  A grand defiance round the moveless shores,
And vocal grown the Mountain's silent head:
      Canst thou not yet awaken
  Beneath the funeral cypress? Earth implores
Thy presence for her son; — why art thou dead?

V.

I do but rave: for it is better thus.
  Were once thy starry nature given to mine,
In the one life which would encircle us
  My voice would melt, my soul be lost in thine.
Better to bear the far sublimer pain
  Of Thought that has not ripened into speech,
To hear in silence Truth and Beauty sing
      Divinely to the brain;
  For thus the Poet at the last shall reach
His own soul's voice, nor crave a brother's string.

SICILIAN WINE.

I 'VE drunk Sicilia's crimson wine!
The blazing vintage pressed
From grapes on Etna's breast,
What time the mellowing autumn sun did shine :
I 've drunk the wine !
I feel its blood divine
Poured on the sluggish tide of mine,
Till, kindling slow,
Its fountains glow
With the light that swims
On their trembling brims,
And a molten sunrise floods my limbs !

What do I here ?
I 've drunk the wine,
And lo ! the bright blue heaven is clear
Above the ocean's bluer sphere,

Seen through the long arcades of pine,
Inwoven and arched with vine!
The glades are green below;
The temple shines afar;
Above, old Etna's snow
Sparkles with many an icy star:
I see the mountain and its marble wall,
Where gleaming waters fall
And voices call,
Singing and calling
Like chorals falling
Through pearly doors of some Olympian hall,
Where Love holds bacchanal.

Sicilian wine! Sicilian wine!
Summer, and Music, and Song divine
Are thine,—all thine!
A sweet wind over the roses plays;
The wild bee hums at my languid ear;
The mute-winged moth serenely strays
On the downy atmosphere,
Like hovering Sleep, that overweighs
My lids with his shadow, yet comes not near.
Who'll share with me this languor?
With me the juice of Etna sip?
Who press the goblet's lip

Refusing mine the while with love's enchanting anger?
Would I were young Adonis now!
With what an ardor bold
Within my arms I'd fold
Fair Aphrodite of Idalian mould,
And let the locks that hide her gleaming brow
Fall o'er my shoulder as she lay
With the fair swell of her immortal breast
Upon my bosom pressed,
Giving Olympian thrills to its enamored clay!

Bacchus and Pan have fled:
No heavy Satyr crushes with his tread
The verdure of the meadow ground,
But in their stead
The Nymphs are leading a bewildering round,
Vivid and light, as o'er some flowering rise
A dance of butterflies,
Their tossing hair with slender lilies crowned,
And greener ivy than o'erran
The brows of Bacchus and the reed of Pan!

I faint, I die:
The flames expire,
That made my blood a fluid fire:
Steeped in delicious weariness I lie.

O, lay me in some pearlèd shell,
Soft-balanced on the rippling sea,
Where sweet, cheek-kissing airs may wave
Their fresh wings over me ;
Let me be wafted with the swell
Of Nereid voices ; let no billow rave
To break the cool green crystal of the sea ;
For I will wander free
Past the blue islands and the fading shores,
To Calpè and the far Azores,
And still beyond, and wide away
Beneath the dazzling wings of tropic day,
Where, on unruffled seas,
Sleep, dragon-watched, the green Hesperides.

The Triton's trumpet calls :
I hear, I wake, I rise :
The sound peals up the skies,
And mellowed Echo falls
In answer back from Heaven's cerulean walls.
Give me the lyre that Orpheus played upon
Or bright Hyperion, —
Nay, rather come, thou of the mighty bow,
Come thou below,
Leaving thy steeds unharnessed go !
Sing as thou wilt, my voice shall dare to follow,

And I will sun me in thine awful glow,
Divine Apollo!
Then thou thy lute shalt twine
With Bacchic tendrils of the glorious vine.
That gave Sicilian wine:
And henceforth when the breezes run
Over its clusters, ripening in the sun,
The leaves shall speak of thee,
Recalling from thy lute its melody,
And I, that quaff, am free
To mount thy car and ride the heavens with thee!

SUMMER'S BACCHANAL.

Fill the cup from some secretest fountain,
Under granite ledges, deep and low,
Where the crystal vintage of the mountain
Runs in foam from dazzling fields of snow!

Some lost stream, that in a woodland hollow
Coils, to sleep its weariness away,
Shut from prying stars, that fain would follow,
In the emerald glooms of hemlock spray.

Fill, dear friend, a goblet cool and sparkling
As the sunlight of October morns, —
Not for us the crimson wave, that darkling
Stains the lips of olden drinking-horns!

We will quaff, beneath the noontide glowing,
  Draughts of nectar, sweet as faery dew;
Couched on ferny banks, where light airs blowing,
  Shake the leaves between us and the blue.

We will pledge, in breathless, long libation,
  All we have been, or have sworn to be,—
Fame, and Joy, and Love's dear adoration,—
  Summer's lusty bacchanals are we!

Fill again, and let our goblets, clashing,
  Stir the feathery ripples on the brim:
Let the light, within their bosoms flashing,
  Leap like youth to every idle limb!

Round the white roots of the fragrant lily
  And the mossy hazels, purple-stained,
Once the music of these waters chilly
  Gave return for all the sweetness drained.

How that rare, delicious, woodland flavor
  Mocked my palate in the fever hours,
When I pined for springs of coolest savor,
  As the burning Earth for thunder-showers!

In the wave, that through my maddened dreaming
  Flowed to cheat me, fill the cups again!
Drink, dear friend, to life which is not seeming, —
  Fresh as this to manhood's heart and brain!

Fill, fill high! and while our goblets, ringing,
  Shine with vintage of the mountain-snow,
Youth shall bid his Fountain, blithely springing,
  Brim our souls to endless overflow!

STORM-LINES.

When the rains of November are dark on the hills, and
the pine-trees incessantly roar
To the sound of the wind-beaten crags, and the floods
that in foam through their black channels pour:

When the breaker-lined coast stretches dimly afar,
through the desolate waste of the gale,
And the clang of the sea-gull at nightfall is heard from
the deep, like a mariner's wail:

When the gray sky drops low, and the forest is bare,
and the laborer is housed from the storm,
And the world is a blank, save the light of his home
through the gust shining redly and warm: —

Go thou forth, if the brim of thy heart with its tropical
fulness of life overflow, —
If the sun of thy bliss in the zenith is hung, and no
shadow reminds thee of woe!

Leave the home of thy love; leave thy labors of fame;
in the rain and the darkness go forth,
When the cold winds unpausingly wail as they drive
from the cheerless expanse of the North.

Thou shalt turn from the cup that was mantling before;
thou shalt hear the eternal despair
Of the hearts that endured and were broken at last,
from the hills and the sea and the air!

Thou shalt hear how the Earth, the maternal, laments
for the children she nurtured with tears, —
How the forest but deepens its wail and the breakers
their roar, with the march of the years!

Then the gleam of thy hearth-fire shall dwindle away,
and the lips of thy loved ones be still;
And thy soul shall lament in the moan of the storm,
sounding wide on the shelterless hill.

All the woes of existence shall stand at thy heart, and
the sad eyes of myriads implore,
In the darkness and storm of their being, the ray,
streaming out through thy radiant door.

Look again: how that star of thy Paradise dims,
through the warm tears, unwittingly shed;—
Thou art man, and a sorrow so bitterly wrung never
fell on the dust of the Dead!

Let the rain of the midnight beat cold on thy cheek,
and the proud pulses chill in thy frame,
Till the love of thy bosom is grateful and sad, and
thou turn'st from the mockery of Fame!

Take with humble acceptance the gifts of thy life; let
thy joy touch the fountain of tears;
For the soul of the Earth, in endurance and pain, gath-
ers promise of happier years!

A PRAYER.

HEAVEN, send not yet thy messenger!
Thy crystal courts are trod
By angels who resembled her,
Ere they were called to God.
They walk thy floors of starry gold,
Choiring thine awful space,
When round their brows the white wings fold
Before the Father's face.
Their myriads fill thy shining sea,
But Earth has one alone for me.

O, leave her, Heaven! she will not make
Thy bowers more bright and fair,
Nor bid a sweeter harp awake
In thy melodious air;
She will not weave a brighter crown
Of amaranth, on thy shore,
Than cast thy burning seraphs down
When mutely they adore:
But she can bid me hear thy streams
And see thy glory in my dreams.

Not yet! Thy call should welcome be
  As sleep to weary eyes,
Nor leave behind, in mockery,
  A pang that never dies:
Should touch the heart like harpings loud,
  White wings and waving hair,
Not with a blast that leaves it bowed
  In terror and despair.
Thy life is peace, thy world is bliss:
Spare thou my only joy in this!

THE TWO VISIONS.

Through days of toil, through nightly fears,
A vision blessed my heart for years;
And so secure its features grew,
My heart belived the blessing true.

I saw her there, a household dove,
In consummated peace of love,
And sweeter joy and saintlier grace
Breathed o'er the beauty of her face:

The joy and grace of love at rest,
The fireside music of the breast,
When vain desires and restless schemes
Sleep, pillowed on our early dreams.

Nor her alone: beside her stood,
In gentler types, our love renewed;
Our separate beings one, in Birth, —
The darling miracles of Earth.

The mother's smile, the children's kiss,
And home's serene, abounding bliss;
The fruitage of a life that bore
But idle summer blooms before:

Such was the vision, far and sweet,
That, still beyond Time's lagging feet,
Lay glimmering in my heart for years,
Dim with the mist of happy tears.

That vision died, in drops of woe,
In blotting drops, dissolving slow:
Now, toiling day and sorrowing night,
Another vision fills my sight.

A cold mound in the winter snow;
A colder heart at rest below;
A life in utter loneness hurled,
And darkness over all the world.

134

My heart, a bird with broken wing,
Deserted by its mate of Spring,
Droops, shivering, while the chill winds blow
And fill the nest of Love with snow.

SONGS AND SONNETS.

STORM SONG.

THE clouds are scudding across the moon,
  A misty light is on the sea ;
The wind in the shrouds has a wintry tune,
  And the foam is flying free.

Brothers, a night of terror and gloom
  Speaks in the cloud and gathering roar :
Thank God, He has given us broad sea-room,
  A thousand miles from shore.

Down with the hatches on those who sleep !
  The wild and whistling deck have we ;
Good watch, my brothers, to-night we 'll keep,
  While the tempest is on the sea !

Though the rigging shriek in his terrible grip
  And the naked spars be snapped away,
Lashed to the helm, we 'll drive our ship
  In the teeth of the whelming spray!

Hark! how the surges o'erleap the deck!
  Hark! how the pitiless tempest raves!
Ah, daylight will look upon many a wreck
  Drifting over the desert waves.

Yet, courage, brothers! we trust the wave,
  With God above us, our guiding chart:
So, whether to harbor or ocean-grave,
  Be it still with a cheery heart!

SONG.

I PLUCKED for thee the wilding rose
  And wore it on my breast,
And there, till daylight's dusky close,
  Its silken cheek was pressed ;
Its desert breath was sweeter far
  Than palace-rose could be,
Sweeter than all Earth's blossoms are,
  But that thou gav'st to me.

I kissed its leaves, in fond despite
  Of lips that failed my own,
And Love recalled that sacred night
  His blushing flower was blown.
I vowed, no rose should rival mine,
  Though withered now, and pale,
Till those are plucked, whose white buds twine
  Above thy bridal veil.

SONG.

Upon a fitful dream of passion
The music stole :
As wild a strain as Joy could fashion
Or Love control,
And on its waves of sweet expression
Was rocked my soul.

It seemed a sea-born music, floating
The blue waves o'er,
Like that which charms the mermaid's boating
By moonlit shore,
In every dying fall denoting
The strains in store.

Now came, like Summer's wind of sweetness,
    Its fanning streams;
Thought, buoyed upon its wing of fleetness,
    Shed fairer beams ;
It gave the rapture of completeness
    To Fancy's dreams.

O, far beyond the best revealing
    Of Poesy,
All things the soul from torture stealing
    It seemed to be,
Yet most, thou Child of Love and Feeling,
    The thought of thee!

THE WAVES.

I.

CHILDREN are we
Of the restless sea,
Swelling in anger or sparkling in glee ;
We follow our race,
In shifting chase,
Over the boundless ocean-space !
Who hath beheld where the race begun ?
Who shall behold it run ?
Who shall behold it run ?

II.

When the smooth airs keep
Their noontide sleep,
We dimple the cheek of the dreaming deep ;
When the rough winds come
From their cloudy home,

At the tap of the hurricane's thunder-drum,
Deep are the furrows of wrath we plow,
Ridging his darkened brow!
Ridging his darkened brow!

III.

Over us born,
The unclouded Morn
Trumpets her joy with the Triton's horn,
And sun and star
By the thousand are
Orbed in our glittering, near and far:
And the splendor of Heaven, the pomp of Day,
Shine in our laughing spray!
Shine in our laughing spray!

IV.

We murmur our spell
Over sand and shell;
We girdle the reef with a combing swell;
And bound in the vice
Of the Arctic ice,
We build us a palace of grand device,—
Walls of crystal and splintered spires,
Flashing with diamond fires!
Flashing with diamond fires!

V.

In the endless round
Of our motion and sound,
The inmost dwelling of Beauty is found,
And with voice of strange
And solemn change,
The elements speak in our world-wide range,
Harping the terror, the might, the mirth,
Sorrows and hopes of Earth!
Sorrows and hopes of Earth!

SONG.

FROM the bosom of ocean I seek thee,
  Thou lamp of my spirit afar,
As the seaman, adrift in the darkness,
  Looks up for the beam of his star;
And when on the moon-lighted water
  The spirits of solitude sleep,
My soul, in the light of thy beauty,
  Lies hushed as the waves of the deep.

As the shafts of the sunrise are broken
  Far over the glittering sea,
Thou hast dawned on the waves of my dreaming,
  And each thought has a sparkle of thee.
And though, with the white sail distended,
  I speed from the vanishing shore,
Thou wilt give to the silence of ocean
  The spell of thy beauty the more.

MARCH.

THE chill March winds are blowing
  Across the gusty tide,
And white ships, seaward going,
  On the swaying surges glide.

I hear a soul of sorrow
  In the voice of wind and wave ;
And would their wail to-morrow
  Might mingle o'er my grave !

Beneath thecheerless gloaming
  The hills lie brown and bare,
And the frosty Night is coming
  To sit in sadness there.

My life is bleak and withered
  As those dark uplands are;
Yet, through the cloud-racks gathered,
  Shines out the Evening Star!

CRICKET SONG.

WELCOME with thy clicking, cricket!
    Clicking songs of sober mirth;
Autumn, stripping field and thicket,
    Brings thee to my hearth,
Where thy clicking shrills and quickens,
While the mist of twilight thickens.

Lately, by the garden wicket,
    Where the thick grass grew unclipt,
And the rill beside thee, cricket,
    Silver-trickling slipt,
Thou, in mid-day's silent glitter,
Mocked the flickering linnet's twitter.

Now thou art, my cheerful cricket,
    Nimble quickener of my song;
Not a thought but thou shalt nick it
    In thy lowly tongue,
And my clock, the moments ticking,
Is thy constant clicking, clicking.

No annoy, good-humored cricket,
    With thy trills is ever blent;
Spleen of mine, how dost thou trick it
    To a calm content!
So, by thicket, hearth, or wicket,
Click thy little lifetime, cricket!

THE FOUNTAIN IN WINTER.

THE Northern winds are raw and cold,
And whistle o'er the frozen mould ;
The gusty branches lash the wall
With icicles that snap and fall.

There is no light on earth to-day ;
The very sky is blank and gray,
Yet still the fountain's quivering shaft
Leaps as if Spring around it laughed.

The drops that strike the frozen mould
Make all the garden doubly cold,
And with a chill and shivering pain
I hear the fall of sleety rain.

The music that, in beamy May,
Told of an endless holiday,
With surly Winter's wailings blent,
Becomes his dreariest instrument.

The water's blithe and sparkling voice,
That all the summer said, "Rejoice!"
Now pours upon the bitter air
The hollow laughter of despair.

So, when the flowers of Life lie dead
Beneath a darker winter's tread,
The songs that once gave Joy a soul
Bring to the heart its heaviest dole.

The fresh delight that leaped and sung
The fragrant bowers of Youth among,
But gives to Sorrow colder tears
And laughs to mock our clouded years.

WORDSWORTH.

I SAW thee not, what time mine eyes beheld
Far-off Helvellyn skirt the misty sea,
When wild Manx waters foamed and tumbled free
Around my keel: I saw thee not, when swelled
Beyond Northumbrian moors the soft blue line
Of mountain chains that look on Windermere;
Yet was it joy to know thy paths so near,
Thy voice on all those hills, O Bard divine!
But I shall see thee where thou sittest now,
Musing, uplift o'er deeps of diamond air,
And I shall feel the splendor of thy brow
Thrown on the scanty wreath that binds my hair,
As, looking down benignly on my place,
Thou read'st the worship in my lifted face.

SONNET.

TO G. H. B.

You comfort me as one that, knowing Fate,
Would paint her visage kinder than you deem ;
You say, my only bliss that is no dream
She clouds, but makes not wholly desolate.
Ah, Friend ! your heart speaks words of little weight
To veil that sadder knowledge, learned in song,
And 'gainst your solace Grief has made me strong :
The Gods are jealous of our low estate ;
They give not Fame to Love, nor Love to Fame ;
Power cannot taste the joy the humble share,
Nor holy Beauty breathe in Luxury's air,
And all in darkness Genius feeds his flame.
We build and build, poor fools ! and all the while
Some Demon works unseen, and saps the pile.

NOTE.

MON-DA-MIN; OR, THE ROMANCE OF MAIZE. — For the Indian legend embodied in this poem, the author is indebted to the very curious and valuable "Algic Researches" of Mr. Schoolcraft. He has added nothing to the simple and beautiful story of the Origin of Maize, as there related, — a story which charmed him the more, from its unexpected grace and symmetry, in the midst of so many grotesque and exaggerated forms of tradition.

www.ingramcontent.com/pod-product-compliance
Lightning Source LLC
LaVergne TN
LVHW021400110826
845150LV00007B/1730

9781425512569